VOTE POWER

VOTE POWER

HOW TO WORK FOR THE PERSON YOU WANT ELECTED

William T. Murphy, Jr.
and Edward Schneier

ANCHOR BOOKS

Anchor Press / Doubleday
Garden City, New York

Anchor Books Edition: 1974
Copyright © 1970 by The Movement for a New Congress
(Palmer Hall, Princeton, N.J.)

Copyright © 1974 by William T. Murphy, Jr., and
Edward Schneier
All Rights Reserved
Printed in the United States of America
First Edition

Library of Congress Cataloging in Publication Data

Murphy, William T.
  Vote power.

  Revised and expanded version of Vote power, published in 1970,
entered under the Movement for a New Congress.
  Includes bibliographical references.
  1. Electioneering—United States—Handbooks, manuals, etc.
2. Political participation—United States—Handbooks, manuals, etc.
I. Schneier, Edward V., joint author. II. Movement for a New
Congress. Vote power. III. Title.
JK2283.M87 1974   329'.00973   73–13281
ISBN 0-385-09577-5
Library of Congress Catalog Card Number 73–13281

CONTENTS

	Preface	vii
CHAPTER 1.	Working Toward a New Congress	1
CHAPTER 2.	Power in Congress	40
CHAPTER 3.	What Can Volunteer Activity Mean? A Case Study of 1970	61
CHAPTER 4.	Getting Started in Electoral Politics	76
CHAPTER 5.	Adding New Voters to the Rolls	101
CHAPTER 6.	Winning Votes	118
CHAPTER 7.	The Economics and Planning of Political Campaigns	137
CHAPTER 8.	Propaganda, Intelligence, and Research	162
CHAPTER 9.	Following Through	186
APPENDIX A	The Ninety-nine Most Marginal House Districts	196
APPENDIX B	The Leadership of the 93rd Congress as of November 1973	200
APPENDIX C	Registration Laws and Absentee Balloting Procedures in the Fifty States	204

PREFACE

Millions of Americans are working for peace, justice, and other worthy causes. Most of these good people are wasting their time. In politics, sincerity, dedication, and virtue are not enough. No prizes are given for running second in an election or for being a nice guy. If nice guys and girls are to win elections—and winning is the name of the game—they must know what they are doing, why they are doing it, and how they can work most effectively to achieve their goals.

This book tells the average citizen how he or she can most effectively participate in the political process. It is both a how-to-do-it manual and a book which explains why some techniques are more valuable than others. It provides both mundane insights into the nuts and bolts of campaigning and long-range perspectives on the viability of our system of representative government. It is a citizen's guide to the art of the politically practical.

The first *Vote Power* was prepared in 1970 for the Movement for a New Congress, a campus-based organization, created in the wake of the 1970 Cambodia bombings and the Kent State killings, in an attempt to mobilize massive grass-roots volunteer efforts to elect a new Congress. This revised and expanded *Vote Power* benefits, we hope, both from the successes and failures of the movement and from the experiences we gained as active participants in it. Although it is directed primarily at those who share our commitments to the causes of peace, racial justice, and the reordering of national priorities, this edition of *Vote Power* should prove equally useful to all citizens, regardless of political persuasion, who wish to be more effective politically. And although our concern is chiefly with Congress, the general principles, proposals, and techniques described here should prove applicable to all campaigns.

In the wake of Watergate, political cynicism is reaching an all-time high. No lecture on democratic theory is going to convince many Americans that corruption is not a part and parcel of the electoral process. But cynicism, doubt, remorse, and despair are wasted and self-serving emotions unless they work as incentives to act. No matter how badly one smarts from past failures, betrayals, and defeats, there is realistically no alternative but to try again. For those who are committed to social goals of any kind, "The real choice," as Michael Walzer puts it,

> is between two kinds of politics, both of which have conventional names, though they can each be pursued in a variety of irregular ways. The two kinds are pressure politics and electoral politics, and I am inclined to think that there are no other kinds. To choose pressure politics means to try to influence those people who already hold power, who sit in official seats, who may even be responsible for the outrages against which the movement is aimed. To choose electoral politics is to try to dislodge those people and plant others in their seats. . . . Of course, the two choices overlap in important ways . . . but it is worth emphasizing the two simply because they exhaust the range: changing the policies men make and changing the men who make policies. Changing the political system within which policy is made is rarely a real option for citizen activists.[1]

This is a book about electoral rather than pressure politics. We do not ignore the latter, indeed, we have quite a bit to say about monitoring Congress, about keeping elected officials honest, about making Congress more effective, and about following through after the election. But whatever the social goals which motivate people to go into politics, the best way to achieve those goals is to elect candidates who share them or to scare hell out of those who do not. Some politicians are shrewd. Some are obtuse. Some are corrupt. All know how to count votes. Nothing could be more important to the future of American society than the way in which those votes are distributed on the first Tuesday following the first Monday of November. On election night they don't count the issues, they count votes. And between elections, politicians don't look back, they think about their next first Tuesdays.

Books on electoral politics and campaigns fill a good-sized bookcase. Some are learned tomes on voting behavior and campaign organization. Many are anecdotal accounts of how some self-designated celebrity did what for whom. Many are specialized manuals on the importance of whatever product is being sold: polls, computers, advance work, TV spots, campaign consultants, management efficiency, or what have you. This book is a little of all three. As professional political scientists, we have tried to bring some of the concepts, theories, and insights of the scholarly literature to bear on problems of practical politics. As people who have been involved in a number of actual campaigns, we cannot help but bring our personal observations into the analysis. And the book does have a special focus: we are concerned primarily with the role of citizen-activists, with how the ordinary citizen can best use his or her good sense and human capabilities in order to participate effectively in electoral politics.

Every candidate will have his or her own ideas about the best ways of arranging the technical details of the campaign. It is not our purpose in this book to debate the relative merits of 3-by-5 as opposed to 4-by-7 cards. There are as many ways to run campaigns as to skin cats; and we are not about to delimit lines of organizational orthodoxy. What we have tried to do is to explain in general terms the ways in which volunteers can maximize their impact on the political process. Candidates can and do make mistakes; but it is better as a rule to allow those mistakes to stand than to have every Tom, Dick, Harry, and Maude in the organization questioning every fundamental decision that is made.

Our focus is on Congress. In Chapter 1 we have tried to justify this orientation and to explain what ordinary citizens can do to help make Congress more effective. Surely there is much to be done. As former Congressman Allard K. Lowenstein (D., New York) wrote recently, "Many political institutions sacrifice efficiency for democracy, or democracy for efficiency. Congress sacrifices both to achieve neither."[2]

The need for a Congress that is both more efficient and more democratic, that is capable of effectively balancing and checking the growing power of the White House and the bureaucracy, is clear and urgent. It is trite but true, however, that it is up to the people to decide whether or not Congress will change. There are, as we hope to show in Chapter 1, some important stirrings of revival and reform on Capitol Hill. They need public nourishment. And the balance of power in Congress, we also try to show, is precarious. By turning around the electoral outcome in a relatively small number of marginal districts, it is conceivable that the fundamental orientation of Congress as an institution can be turned around as well.

But before attempting to turn an institution around, it might be useful to know something about it. To say that Congress is not a very well-understood institution is to put the case mildly. The average American knows next to nothing about Congress. Surveys have shown, for example, that about half of the American people do not even know the name of their representative in Washington. Even the well-informed, moreover, tend to have distorted views. This problem is in part the fault of the press. Journalists look for the sensational, the off-beat, and the bizarre. The day-to-day workings of Congress, the inside struggles for power, the realities of effective lawmaking make poor copy and are hence obscured from all but a handful of the American people. It is our purpose in Chapter 2 to describe the *Realpolitik* of Capitol Hill.

Chapter 3 is basically a case study of the 1970 congressional campaign. Although our focus is on the efforts of student campaigners, our purpose is to show more generally what volunteer activists can and cannot do.

In Chapters 4–8 we deal with the how and why of grass-roots activism—from choosing candidates and organizing a campaign to registration, canvassing, fund raising, publicity, polls, and research. These chapters combine detailed descriptions of how to do it with analysis of the reasons for preferring certain techniques to others.

Finally, in Chapter 9 we offer some suggestions for following through on the efforts launched during a campaign: how to keep tabs on your representative in Congress and make him a more effective legislator. How to continue to be an active force in the American political process. The appendices provide facts and figures designed to help the reader evaluate more fully the work of Congress.

Any individual's personal influence in a large arena is likely to be small. Your vote, in the typical congressional district, is likely to be worth about $\frac{1}{150,000}$th of the total cast. But the individual's influence and impact can be extended dramatically through campaign activity. People will vote for a candidate for many reasons—they like his or her stands on the issues, they are distantly related to his brother-in-law's second cousin—but the most compelling reason of all is simply that somebody whose opinions they respect asked them to. There is no substitute for face-to-face contact with the voters. And there is no substitute for active volunteers

who are informed, articulate, and know what they are doing. It is our hope that this book will enable and encourage
its readers to assume that role and thus to enhance their
power as citizens.

The 1970 edition of *Vote Power* was a hastily prepared,
photo-offset handbook designed to meet the immediate needs
of the Movement for a New Congress. Although considerably
more time and thought went into the present volume, our
debt to the Movement is substantial. To Gary Orfield, who
made the Movement for a New Congress a viable organization, and to Henry Bienen, who made it work, we extend both
our thanks and our respect. Above all, to the thousands of
students and others who worked in the 1970 campaign and
who, we hope, profited from this book, we owe our inspira-
tion.

More tangible debts of gratitude are owed to those who
contributed their insights and writings to both editions of this
book. For the first edition we owe particular debts to Henry
and Leigh Bienen, Janice B. Schneier, and the staff of the
National Office of the Movement for a New Congress. The
comments and suggestions of Stanley Kelley, Jr., and Matthew Reese were very helpful. Errors of omission and commission in this revised edition, we would like to think, are
somebody else's fault. Both tradition and honesty, however,
compel us to take such blame upon ourselves and to acknowl-
edge our thanks to the following: David Harrop, our editor
at Doubleday, harassed us so persistently, and Georgiana
Remer did so thorough a job of copy-editing the manuscript
that it is only in retrospect that we can appreciate how much
we owe them. Joyce Murphy is to be thanked not only for
putting up with our somewhat unorthodox writing habits, but
for combining her talents with those of Karen Kerns, Elaine
Ugolnik, and Carol Sherman in converting our scribbles into
readable copy. Lianne Fleisher made useful editorial suggestions. Congressmen John Brademus, Frank Thompson, and
Morris Udall, along with former Speaker of the House John

McCormack, offered important help and advice, as did the League of Women Voters. And our students at Brown University and the City College of New York served at once as editorial advisers, critics, guinea pigs, and inspirations. It is to them, and to the hopes and aspirations they embody for a New Congress and a New Society, that this book is dedicated.

We wrote the first *Vote Power* in an environment of public outrage and despair—particularly manifested on college and university campuses—over the invasion of Cambodia and the shootings at Kent State University and Jackson State College. As we prepare our final revisions for this second edition, a similar atmosphere of crisis prevails, this time growing out of concern for the very institutions of our government itself and no longer confined, we might add, to the academic community. One runs the risk, in times such as these, of being overwhelmed by events, of having one's words sound anachronistic even as they are written. It has been a relatively easy matter to change the tense of the verbs relating to Spiro Agnew and to change his title from Vice President to *former* Vice President. But now the President himself is in serious trouble, and it is increasingly problematic—to use the Chief Executive's own inimitable phrase—whether we will "have Richard Nixon to kick around any more."

But although we have used Mr. Nixon as a case in point, the deeper institutional problems we raise in Chapters 1 and 2 were neither of his creation nor in his capacity fully to control. The problems of Congress remain problems, whether the President is impeached, forced to resign, or manages to tough it through. The contest for power between the Congress and the President is not a zero-sum game where one side necessarily gains at the other's expense. A weakened and discredited President does not *ipso facto* create a strengthened and revitalized Congress. Indeed, what is to be feared most, in these dark fall days of 1973, is that the American Congress and the American people may be lulled, by the vicissitudes of

Mr. Nixon's fortunes and misfortunes, into thinking that some
of the deeper problems of our system of separated powers
have been resolved.

William T. Murphy, Jr.

November 1973   *Edward Schneier*

NOTES

1. Michael Walzer, *Political Action: A Practical Guide to
   Movement Politics* (Chicago: Quadrangle Books,
   1971), pp. 25–26.
2. Allard K. Lowenstein, foreword to Jeff Fishel, *Party and
   Opposition* (New York: McKay, 1973), p. ix.

VOTE POWER

CHAPTER 1

WORKING TOWARD A NEW CONGRESS

Seldom before today has American history seen such wide-spread cynicism and discontent with our governmental institutions, with the tone and direction of public policies, and with the state of our politics. Percentage turnout in national elections has been declining steadily since 1960. Especially among minorities—non-whites, the young, the poor—there is a strong and growing dissatisfaction with the institutions of American politics. The Watergate caper and the revelations and events that flowed out of it appeared to many Americans not as aberrations but rather as symbols of "politics as usual" in the United States.

If there is any single institution in our system which has served as a focal point for despair it is Congress. It is here that the gap between traditional ideas and political realities seems most pronounced. It is here, and particularly in the House of Representatives, that the frustrations of reformers run deepest, that the fear of change seems greatest, and that the forces of reaction seem strongest. Set against the back-drop of a world-wide decline in the power of legislative assemblies, the signs of congressional decline would seem to have particularly ominous connotations.

WHAT POWERS DOES CONGRESS HAVE?

To describe this era as one of executive force is commonplace. In both foreign and domestic policies, the executive branch has become, in Richard Neustadt's words, "the regular, accustomed source of all major initiatives." Yet the Congress of the United States remains the strongest legislative body in the world. Its potential powers are vast. An assertive, bold, and dynamic Congress, one that both checks and activates the executive, one that both responds to and anticipates social change, is essential to the future health and welfare of our society.

Recent sessions of Congress have raised expectations that the legislative branch of the federal government is moving toward a reassertion of its constitutional role in the area of foreign policy and toward a reaffirmation of its responsibility for ordering domestic priorities. The repeal of the Gulf of Tonkin resolution, the adoption of legislation to halt the bombing of Cambodia, the Ervin Committee's relentless pursuit of the Watergate inquiry, along with aggressive attempts to reassert control over budgetary decisions offer encouraging signs. But they must be institutionalized and defined if they are to have long-range meaning. Congress must prove that its new aggressiveness is founded in something firmer than the opportunistic desire of its Democratic majority to embarrass a Republican President. For it to do this, its new-found independence must be sanctioned and reinforced by the electorate.

Whatever problems Congress may have, they do not derive from a lack of formal powers. By defining legislative authority in Article I of the Constitution, the founding fathers clearly intended to make Congress the first branch of government. In doing so, they conferred upon Congress "all legislative powers herein granted." They gave it the power of the purse, the power to declare war, to make rules for the government, and to make "all laws which shall be necessary and proper for carrying into execution the foregoing powers." They gave Congress the authority to check the actions of the Executive by requiring senatorial confirmation of major appointments and treaties; by giving Congress the authority to override presidential vetoes; and, in extreme case, by granting the Congress the power to impeach.

Many of these powers have fallen into disuse less by conscious decision than by a subtle erosion of confidence, purpose, and will. As the problems of governing a technological society became more complex, the temptation grew to delegate decision-making authority to the experts and bureaucratic technicians of the executive branch. What began, however, as a logical transfer of policy-initiating roles was subtly transformed into an abdication of decision-making responsibility. The old adage "keep the experts on tap but not on top" was redefined if not repealed. The high (or low) point in these developments was the near-unanimous passage in 1964 of the Gulf of Tonkin Resolution in effect giving President Johnson and his advisers *carte blanche* authority to do as they pleased militarily in Southeast Asia. The formal powers, however, remain. And it is important that they be asserted. For as much as Congress has failed to live up to the responsibilities we would assign it, the bureaucratic alternative seems no more desirable.

CONGRESS VERSUS THE EXECUTIVE

In absolute terms, the power of Congress has not declined. Quite the contrary. Congress today deals with more issues of more importance to all of us than ever before. It handles the biggest budget of any organization in the world, more than a quarter of a trillion dollars, twice what it was a decade ago, more in ten months in 1973 than the combined total for all

federal outlays between 1788 and 1942. It deals with problems that were virtually unheard of just a generation ago:
supersonic transports, nuclear power plants, multinational
corporations, methadone maintenance programs, biodegrad-
able detergents.

In its relations with the executive branch, however, the
powers of Congress have clearly declined. Congress has
more power but less control than ever before, a smaller share
of a much bigger pie. But there are strong signs of congressional revival, particularly with regard to problems of foreign
policy, access to information, and control of the purse. In all
three of these areas Congress seems on the verge of reasserting
its constitutional powers; but the main battles are still to be
fought.

The war powers issue has received the most popular attention. It is not a new one. During the nineteenth century,
Presidents regularly used their constitutional authority as
Commanders-in-Chief to commit American troops for the sup-
pression of piracy, for the protection of American lives and
property abroad, and for other reasons. But the powers of
the President were sharply limited in the nineteenth century
by the simple fact that there was not a very large standing
army or navy to command.

> At the time of the ratification of the Constitution the
> United States Army consisted of 719 officers and men.
> Our armed forces increased to some 20,000 by 1840, to
> 28,000 on the eve of the Civil War and to 38,000 by
> 1890. Even in 1915, with the world locked in mortal
> combat, the armed forces of the United States were less
> than 175,000. With the worst will, there was little that
> Presidents could do with these forces. Now we have a
> wholly new situation. Not only do we keep some three
> million men under arms at all times—since 1951 the
> number has rarely fallen below that—but we have the
> greatest and most formidable armaments that any nation
> ever commanded.[1]

As the United States became a major military power, major conflicts—the two World Wars—were fought with congressional consent; but Presidents continued to engage in more limited encounters—particularly in Latin America—on their own initiatives.

Since World War II, the United States has fought major wars in Korea and Vietnam and engaged in more limited military encounters in all parts of the world without declarations of war by Congress. President Truman's right to intervene in Korea was sharply questioned by Senator Robert A. Taft (Ohio) and other conservative Republicans in 1950, but the war powers issue died out with the signing of a cease-fire agreement in 1953.

A decade of American involvement in Vietnam, however, has finally brought the issue to a head. In 1969 the Senate adopted S. 85, declaring as the sense of the Senate that national commitments could be made only "from affirmative action taken by the legislative and executive branches." In 1970 both houses repealed the Gulf of Tonkin Resolution. In 1972 both houses passed war powers bills defining a stronger congressional role; but differences between the House and Senate versions of the bill prevented it from becoming law. Some sort of congressional resolution either defining or elaborating upon the constitutional war-making responsibilities of the President and the Congress is likely to be enacted by the 93rd Congress; but a number of issues remain unresolved.

One of the most important of these is the problem of executive agreements. The line between so-called "executive agreements" and formal treaties has never been clearly defined, except insofar as the former do not require Senate approval. Presidents, with increasing frequency, have bypassed the Senate by using executive agreements in their dealings with foreign governments. The following table illustrates dramatically the change[2]:

	Treaties	Executive Agreements
1789–1939	800	1200
1940–1960	300	2000
1963–1967	47	1136

Even this table understates the case by including only those executive agreements which have been acknowledged. As a Senate subcommittee chaired by Stuart Symington (D., Missouri) discovered in 1969, however, many of these arrangements are made behind closed doors. The Eisenhower, Kennedy, Johnson, and Nixon administrations, for example, all signed agreements pledging the United States to "instantly repel" any armed attack on the Philippines. Four Presidents, in this case, had not only bypassed the treaty-making process but had neglected to inform the Congress that such agreements existed.[3]

There are legitimate reasons for the withholding of information. National security may dictate the withholding of information on the deployment of troops, specific battle plans, etc. Certain internal memorandums and files of Executive agencies should also be "off limits" to the public, and perhaps to Congress. As long as the Federal Bureau of Investigation, for example, continues to compile elaborate dossiers that contain unevaluated charges against individuals and as long as the Civil Service Commission keeps similar dossiers, a respect for civil liberties demands that these files remain confidential. Similarly, pending but incomplete federal investigations of corporations must be kept confidential in order to guard against undeserved economic damages or windfall profits. But there is no doubt that the doctrine of executive privilege and the right to classify documents have been grossly abused. Even in cases where the public's "right to know" is questionable, it is difficult to justify the withholding of information from Congress.

Under a parliamentary system of government, the "question hour" is of long-standing importance. In Britain, members of the governing Cabinet must respond publicly to some 24,000 questions put to them by members of the House of Commons during a single session. "Many a minister," as Bradshaw and Pring say, "has been able to establish his reputation by means of his mastery of the House at Question Time." But ministerial careers have also been destroyed by ineptitude, glaring inefficiencies exposed, and important policy changes instituted as outgrowths of the Question Time. At its best, it "can provide, quickly though briefly, an unceasing stream of up-to-date facts over the whole area of the government's competence."[4]

Committee hearings, in the United States Congress, are a diffused (and sometimes defused) equivalent of the parliamentary Question Time. Some members of the President's Cabinet, it sometimes seems, spend as much time testifying before committees of the House and Senate as they do at their desks. But it is important—indeed vital—to our form of government that they do so. The first law of democratic administration is that bureaucrats must be held publicly accountable for their acts. The growing importance of the White House staff, however, threatens seriously to erode this principle. The roles of special White House adviser Henry M. Kissinger and the nominal Secretary of State, William P. Rogers, were the subjects of many late-night TV jokes. Funny or not, Kissinger's appointment, prior to his being named Secretary of State, was not subject to Senate approval and he had never testified before a congressional committee. The Nixon administration, moreover, has attempted to reorganize the entire upper echelon of government along similar lines. "All this," says the National Committee for an Effective Congress,

is being done in the name of greater efficiency. In fact, the design reproduces that of the Nixon foreign policy apparatus, where the untouchable Dr. Kissinger commands a personal foreign ministry while the accountable

Secretary of State is a ceremonial figure, able to share very little with Congress except frustration. Similar atrophy awaits departments with jurisdiction over natural resources, urban matters, transportation, commerce, health, education, and welfare. Broad domestic and economic policy will be directed by a small group of managers . . . who will operate behind the shield of "Special Presidential Assistant." The chain of command will flow through an inner network of assistant secretaries and bureau chiefs picked from the inner circle of White House loyalists. Cabinet officers will have nothing to do with their selection nor exercise any real authority over them. Thus, instead of the accountable "open government" Mr. Nixon promised the American people, the cabinet system will fade and control will be concentrated in an authoritarian president."[5]

Congress, however, has not only failed to push for greater openness in the executive branch, it has itself also been far from blameless in displaying an excessive zeal for secrecy. A 1972 study in *Congressional Quarterly*, for example, showed that 40 per cent of all committee meetings, including most of those in which bills were actually drafted, were held in secret. There are signs of change. "Teller" votes on the floor are now recorded. Votes in most committees—closely guarded secrets prior to 1970—must now be published. And in 1973 the House voted to make all committee meetings open to the public unless a majority of the committee members specifically voted otherwise. These commitments have not always been honored, but it is clear that the public's access to the work of Congress is greater now than ever before.

The problem of government secrecy is an important one. Congress has become highly dependent upon executive agencies for information, and without good and full information, the quality of legislative work must suffer. But the most serious contemporary issue of legislative-executive relations is the battle for control over the power to spend. As Allen Schick puts it:

The power of the purse is a barometer of legislative vigor and purpose, reflecting the ups and downs in the long contest between Congress and the President for control over spending. To the victor has gone not only financial power but governmental supremacy as well.[6]

It was through its assertion of the power of the purse that Congress was able in 1973 to force a halt in the bombing of Cambodia. It is through this power, more generally, that Congress can determine who gets what, when, and how in the making of public policy.

President Nixon's impoundment, or refusal to spend, more than $11 billion of appropriated funds in 1973 brought the issue to public attention. But it had been building for a long time, and the problem was not simply of the President's making. As Senate Majority Leader Mike Mansfield (D., Montana) put it at the meeting of the Democratic caucus on January 3, 1973:

> The fault lies not in the executive branch but in ourselves in the Congress. We cannot insist upon the power to control expenditures and then fail to do so. If we do not do the job, if we continue to abdicate our constitutional responsibility, the powers of the federal government will have to be recast so that it can be done elsewhere. We must face the fact that an institution, Congress, is not readily equipped to carry out this complex responsibility.[7]

There is a false tendency to regard the President as more capable than the Congress to deal with budgetary problems. In fact the President is probably less capable of paying careful attention to details, of comparing one federal agency's requests to another's. "Why," asks Aaron Wildavsky,

> does the President, who spends perhaps 20 hours a year on the annual budget, seem more rational than the chairman of the House Appropriations Committee, who must spend 2,000 hours on it? Because one is announced by trumpet blasts from on high while the other sounds

more like the Tower of Babel instead of the Heavenly
Chorus. The one budget is made in private and the
other in public. Congressmen see how their budget is
made; knowing what went into it they are, like sausage
makers, afraid of what will come out of it. Unaware of
what has been going on in the Executive Office of the
President, they respect the products more because they
know the ingredients less. Congressmen have come to
prefer other people's errors to their own.[8]

Congress does, however, have good reason to suspect its
own judgment. It has, to begin with, developed no mechanisms for setting priorities or comparing the relative merits of
various expenditures. The classic conflict between guns and
butter is never joined because the two budgets are considered
separately. The essence of setting priorities is comparison:
Is an extra dollar spent on education worth more or less than
an extra dollar for defense? It may be that it is intrinsically
impossible ever to make such comparisons rationally, but the
point is that there is no way now—rational or not—to make
such comparisons. In 1970, for example, the Department of
Interior's budget was approved in July, the Peace Corp's
on December 31.

In 1973 Congress rejected President Nixon's proposal for
setting a rigid ceiling of federal expenditures because it would
delegate to the President the Congress's responsibility for setting priorities. Congress, the President rejoined, was inca-
pable of performing that task. Rather,

A momentum of extravagance is speeded by requirements created by legislative committees sympathetic to
particular and narrow causes. The committees are encouraged by special interest groups and by some executive
branch officials who are more concerned with expansion
of their programs than with total federal spending.[9]

The charge is not completely justified. Even during the Nixon
presidency, Congress has consistently cut rather than aug-

mented the President's budget requests by an average of almost $5 billion a year. In doing so, it has in a sense re-ordered priorities: defense and foreign aid have been cut substantially, while environmental, health, and education programs have been granted more than the President requested. Table 1 shows the magnitude and direction of these actions on major appropriations bills.

Table I

Appropriation Actions, by Bill, for
Fiscal Year 1973

Bill	Total approved (dollars)	Over(+) or under(−) presidential requests (dollars)
1. Legislative	513,788,980	−5,559,919
2. Treasury-Post Office- General government	5,057,827,000	−8,776,000
3. District of Columbia (federal funds)	316,393,000	−26,913,000
4. Interior	2,548,935,300	+21,781,300
5. HUD-Space- Science- Veterans	20,125,951,000	−372,232,000
6. Labor-HEW (H. R. 15417, vetoed)	(39,538,919,500)	(+10,771,286,000)

Bill	Total approved (dollars)	Over (+) or under (−) presidential requests (dollars)
7. Labor-HEW (H. R. 16654, new bill)	30,538,919,500	+1,771,286,000)
8. Agriculture-Environmental and Consumer Protection	13,434,032,700	+481,842,300
9. Public Works-AEC	5,504,914,000	+15,856,000
10. Transportation Advance 1974 appropriation	2,867,937,095 (131,181,000)	+41,244,000
11. Disaster relief (supplemental 1973)	1,587,300,000	+17,500,000
12. Defense	74,372,976,000	−5,221,208,000
13. State-Justice-Commerce-Judiciary	4,681,017,850	−23,308,750
14. Military construction	2,323,403,000	−337,981,000
15. Supplemental 1973	4,933,415,610	−83,125,000

Bill	Total approved (dollars)	Over (+) or under (−) presidential requests (dollars)
16. Foreign assistance	3,652,701,000	−1,510,323,000
	172,459,701,000	−5,322,405,069

SOURCE: Senate Committee on Government Operations, *Improving Congressional Control Over the Budget: A Compendium of Materials,* 93rd Congress, 1st Session (Washington, D.C. Government Printing Office, 1973), p. 193. These figures are as of October 19, 1972.

So Congress does in fact reset priorities, it does in fact have a substantial redistributive impact on the President's budget. But its mechanisms for doing this are badly flawed. Not only does it never look at the budget as a whole, the budget it looks at is not an accurate index of what government does. For fiscal year 1974, the Office of Management and Budget has estimated that 75 per cent of outlays will be "relatively uncontrollable," that is, they cannot be cut or controlled through the traditional appropriations process. Social Security is a good example of an "uncontrollable" item. Congress sets the rates and establishes rules of eligibility (age, earned income, etc.). Once these rates and rules are set, the amount spent in any given year depends entirely upon how many people meet the standards set. If a lot of people retire and few die, Social Security costs will be high; if many die and few retire they will be low. But the point is that the amount paid out to beneficiaries is automatic.

The proportion of the budget characterized as "relatively uncontrollable" has been growing steadily, from $100 billion in 1967 to an estimated $202 billion in the fiscal year 1974. One reason for this growth has been the desire on the part of congressmen on "substantive" committees to bypass the

Appropriations Committees. They can thus avoid what former Secretary of Health, Education and Welfare Elliot Richardson has called the "authorization-appropriation gap." "Historically," said Richardson,

> one set of committees in the House and Senate creates programs and another set actually provides the money for them. The political incentives for a member of an authorizing committee is to pass bills with big price tags —and much publicity—to show he "cares about solving problems." Such an incentive does not apply to members of appropriating committees. Time after time the figures on the price tag are higher than anything the executive branch can in good conscience request, and higher than anything that appropriations committees are willing to provide.
>
> There results, then, an "authorization-appropriation gap"—a gap which has grown by $13 billion. For the public, the authorization-appropriation process has become, in a sense, a shell game. Hopes are raised by attention to the authorizing hoopla, only to be dashed by the less flamboyant hand of the appropriations process.[10]

On all of these issues—war powers, executive agreements, secrecy, the power of the purse—a clear majority in both houses of Congress is prepared to act, but the exact details of the steps to be taken are not clear, many reforms face the strong possibility of presidential vetoes. As the legislative process grinds slowly, it may take years for many changes to be fully implemented. There is a danger, furthermore, that they will simply wither away. The paradox of reform has always been that when the need is most apparent, the votes aren't there, and when the votes are available, the sense of urgency is lacking.

WHAT ARE THE STAKES IN
CONGRESSIONAL ELECTIONS?

The ultimate determinant of what happens on these and other issues is the kind of Congress the people elect in November. Off-year elections are a particularly important barometer of public attitudes. If significant numbers of those who oppose congressional reform are defeated, more will change than the simple mathematics of the vote. The press will speak of a "mandate for change," and those traditionalists who survive will rethink their positions. Elections, in other words, change moods as well as people. Rightly or wrongly, the 1970 elections were interpreted as gauging the strength of the "silent majority." The election of 1972 was seen as a vindication of President Nixon's foreign and domestic policies.

The 1974 elections, to the degree that they are not seen as referendums on Watergate, are going to be viewed as tests of public interest in a revitalized Congress. Numbers are important too, particularly in the House where the liberal-conservative balance is very close. For a variety of reasons, the House for some time has been both the more conservative body and the graveyard of legislative reform. Perhaps its most disgraceful moment was in 1972 when the House voted to surrender to the President all discretion over spending and budget cuts. In a pattern that has become all too familiar, the Senate reversed this domestic Tonkin Resolution by an overwhelming margin. Time and time again, a near-unanimous Senate has been rebuffed by the House in the Senate's attempts to limit presidential power. A bill to require congressional confirmation of presidential appointment to the White House offices or executive directors of the National Security Council, Domestic Council, and Council on International Economic Policy was passed by a 72 to 21 vote in the Senate, but was defeated in the House.

One reason for the Senate's greater liberalism is rooted in the different constituencies of the two bodies. Despite reapportionment, the House remains, in general, a more rural-oriented body. Senators, furthermore, "whose constituencies are entire states, are faced on the whole, with more heterogeneous electorates than are the congressmen, whose constituencies are smaller and likely to be more homogeneous."[11] Senators are politically compelled, in other words, to be more cosmopolitan.

Another important reason for the greater liberalism of the Senate is rooted in historical accident. The Eisenhower recession of 1958 hit farmers hard. It helped elect to the Senate a group of liberal Democrats, like R. Vance Hartke of Indiana, Gale W. McGee of Wyoming, Frank E. Moss of Utah, and Edmund S. Muskie of Maine, whose victories in traditionally Republican states were as significant as they were surprising. Helped by Lyndon Johnson's coattails in 1964 and by their accumulated seniority in 1970, these "class of '58" Democrats form the hard core of liberal strength in the Senate: eighteen of the forty-two northern Democrats in the body. Of the thirty-four senators whose terms expire in 1974, on the other hand, fifteen are Republicans, and five of the nineteen Democrats are from the South. Conservatives will do well to hold their own in the Senate in 1974.

It is in the House, then, that the important political battles of 1974 will be fought. There the margins of victory and defeat on a number of major issues have been close in the 93rd Congress. For example:

—An amendment by Joseph P. Addabbo (D., New York) prohibiting transfers of funds from other programs to support the bombing in Cambodia was sustained by a margin of seven votes.

—An amendment by John B. Anderson (R., Illinois) that would have required a concurrent resolution by both houses to overrule a presidential impoundment of funds, rather than a simple resolution passed by either house, was defeated 206–205. A subsequent effort by Anderson to recommit this bill also failed narrowly, 212–208.

—An amendment to the foreign aid bill by H. R. Gross (R., Iowa) to delete $93 million authorized for selected economic and social development programs failed on a teller vote, 204–203.

Despite President Nixon's overwhelming electoral victory in 1972, an unprecedented pattern of ticket-splitting indicated a decisive affirmation of the public's belief in an independent Congress. But the meaning of that mandate remains unclear: the awesome powers of the modern presidency, the congressional habit of deferring to executive leadership, the size of the President's majority, and the uncertain effects and meanings of the Watergate inquiries have put the Congress into a state of suspended animation. The signs of change are in the air but will remain "blowing in the wind" until the public registers a firm commitment one way or the other.

Clearly there is more at stake in 1974 than 435 seats in the House of Representatives and thirty-four in the Senate. Particularly in these times of political uncertainty, the elections are likely to call the tune of our politics for the next two years and have a dramatic impact on plans and calculations for the presidential campaign in 1976. Leadership in both parties—both symbolic and formal—is also at stake. Who will emerge in both parties as major spokesmen and front runners for the nomination? Will conservative Republicans in the Senate be emboldened to launch another challenge to their Minority Leader, Hugh Scott (Pennsylvania)? Will Democrats continue to support the rather passive leadership styles of Mike Mansfield in the Senate and Carl Albert (Oklahoma) in the House? And what about committee chairmen? Since 1970, ten of twenty-one House committee chairmen have resigned or been defeated. In 1973, moreover, the Democratic party caucus adopted a rule abolishing seniority and requiring the election of all committee chairmen. Will the new rule be used? Will it make a difference in the new Congress?

WHAT STANDS IN THE WAY OF CHANGE?

The answers to some of these questions will be slow to emerge. The Congress that convenes in January 1975 will probably not be radically different from the one that sits in Washington now. Barring plague, natural catastrophe, or a rash of unexpected resignations, two thirds of the Senate's one hundred members will return automatically. A very high percentage of the 435 members of the House of Representatives will be returned by election almost as easily; a basic fact of American politics is that most seats in Congress are safe for the incumbents. Typically, we can expect thirty-eight of 535 senators and representatives to resign or retire during a two-year session, thirteen to die, eleven to be defeated in a party primary, and thirty-one to lose their seats in the November election. Fewer than a hundred, in other words, or about 17 per cent, will fail to be returned—less than half of those because of defeat at the polls. In the context of recent political history, a party shift of more than thirty congressional seats in the November elections must be considered a landslide.

This stability is in part due to the way in which voting district lines are drawn. In states where one party clearly controls the governorship and both houses of the legislature, district lines are drawn with an eye toward party control of the delegation. There are several ways of doing this, even with districts of equal size. By lumping as many Democratic voters as possible into one district, for example, a Republican legislature concedes that seat to the opposition. In doing so, however, it removes Democratic areas from the surrounding districts and may thus make three or four "safe" Republican seats out of districts that previously were marginal. In states where a single party does not have a complete control over reapportionment, the usual "deal" is simply to make the seats of all incumbents of both parties a little more secure. This solution has the added advantage of helping the delegation build seniority in the House of Representatives and thus gain influence for the state in Washington. The net products of these processes are the same, that is, virtually to guarantee most House seats to one party or the other.

Even without a safe district, the advantages of incumbency are enormous. Unlike many of their challengers, incumbent senators and representatives are experienced campaigners. For at least two years they have been able to perform countless services for their constituencies. They have been invited to give scores of commencement addresses, present plaques to Boy Scout heroes, cut ribbons opening new stores, factories, and highways. Their names are constantly in the press. Their staffs in Washington spend much of their time cultivating constituents. They have the use of the franking privilege whereby their official mailings, unlike those of their challengers, are delivered free of charge.

A second disadvantage of reform-oriented candidates in 1974 is that the off-year electorate tends to have a conservative bias. The young and the poor generally have poor voting records as compared with older and more affluent citizens. These differences are even more marked in non-presidential years, when only the best informed and highly motivated are likely to vote.

The third problem is money. Big money in the United States is often used to buy political access. As a rule it goes to those who are already in power. The chairmen of key subcommittees don't even have to ask for contributions from members of groups whose economic destinies they can affect. And although Watergate may have made some contributors wary, the administration in power always has built-in advantage in attracting money.

The financial woes of most challengers are compounded

by a law of self-fulfilling prophecy that seems inherent to our system of campaign finance. Organizations like labor unions, peace groups, or the National Committee for an Effective Congress want to use their resources where they will do the most good. Rather than invest in losing causes, they look at past election returns or marginal districts. This in turn helps make hopeless districts more hopeless, and marginal ones more marginal. It doesn't cost anything to run for Congress; but it costs a lot to run a good campaign and more to win. In most parts of the country, $30,000 is a minimum figure.

Money is also important because it is needed to buy attention. This brings us to the last and most formidable barrier to electoral change—the don't-know-don't-care-don't-understand-don't-bother-me attitude of the typical voter. Even voters with strong commitments to change are not always prepared to act on the basis of that commitment. "Reformers," Boss Plunkitt of Tammany Hall observed at the turn of the century, are "mornin' glories—looked lovely in the mornin' and withered up in a short time, while the regular machines went on flourishin' forever, like fine old oaks."[12] Not all reformers are political morning glories (nor are too many of those fine old oaks still flourishing), but the description comes uncomfortably close to the mark. Campaigning for change is hard work, and the rewards for volunteers are at best intangible.

Many voters, moreover, are not particularly concerned about their congressman's record as a lawmaker. In the words of one House member:

> Unless you can keep constantly in contact with your people, serving them and letting them know what you are doing, you are in a bad way. My experience is that people don't care how I vote on foreign aid, federal aid to education and all those big issues, but they are very much interested in whether I answer their letter and

who is going to be the next rural mail carrier or the next postmaster. Those are things that really count.[13]

In the final analysis, it is the apathy of the electorate combined with attitudes like the one described above that stand as the most formidable barriers to change. Congress could not and would not have conceded power so readily had it not had a silent partner in the American public. For members of Congress, the political pay-off for independence, foresight, initiative, and public-mindedness is often nil, as long as voters tend to be more interested in what favors their representatives have done for them than in what they have done for the nation. The surest road to re-election is to keep the fences mended back home, to answer the mail, to focus on local issues, and to keep a "low profile" on controversial questions. A popular Washington aphorism has it that "a statesman is a retired politician." Whether or not it is true, the role of statesman carries few political rewards. In the words of former Senator Joseph S. Clark (D., Pennsylvania):

> I have made long speeches in the Senate on disarmament, civil rights and the manpower revolution which inspired either a few paragraphs from the wire services or nothing at all in many a paper. . . . But when I have forwarded the announcement of a new post office or a million-dollar contract award, I have been blessed with streamer headlines, even pictures, and once a special box on the front page of the Pottstown *Mercury* headed "Thank You Senator!"[14]

Despite such experiences, Clark continued to devote the bulk of his time to important national issues, in particular to problems of congressional reform. Clark lost his seat in 1968.

First experiences are likely to be particularly discouraging to novice campaigners. Fired by zealous beliefs in a cause or candidate, their encounters with fellow citizens who neither know nor care about issues or offices are like a sharp dash of cold water. Many citizen's first day of campaign activity has also been his last. But Rule 1 of volunteer politics is simple: *Don't get discouraged.* Don't get discouraged if doors are slammed in your face; it happens all the time. Don't get discouraged by the mountains of donkey work that must be done; think what it would cost to hire professional stamp-lickers.

Above all it is important not to be discouraged by perceived defects in the candidate you are working for. Politics necessarily involves compromise. As Michael Walzer says:

> We become political men when we act for public and not private reasons, or at least for public in addition to private reasons, and we imagine our effects in terms of other people as well as ourselves. Political action is action with or for others and while we may think our personal feelings very important (as we all do), they are, in fact, less important than the inevitably impersonal feelings for other people that are involved in acting with this group, for this group, against that group of men and women who we cannot really know.[15]

This is one reason why politics is so often seen as amoral, why political action so often seems to mean selling out on one's moral convictions. It *is* selling out. It is, and must be, the abandonment of the notion that one individual has a monopoly on truth or virtue. It is, in the end, a belief in the rights of the majority, a faith, in the long run, in the ability of the American people to govern themselves. True, the people often need guidance. Principles are important. And if you aren't going to try to help provide some of that guidance, who is?

WHAT ARE THE OPPORTUNITIES FOR WINNING?

Some of the best candidates running in 1974 and 1976 will go down to ignominious defeat. Some of the worst will win handily. Many Americans sincerely believe that the President should have more power, not less; that Congress is, at best, an impediment to effective leadership in these times of trouble. But the opportunities for electing a more responsible Congress are good for at least four reasons.

American politics, to begin with, is in a state of flux.

> Beneath the much-touted recent political reaction and widespread public apathy, there is also a considerable regeneration of American society struggling to break through. Some is on the left, some on the right, and much in the middle, even in the major parties. . . .
>
> The large number of new voters and the high level of independence among them reinforce the probability that a critical passage in the politics of this country is at hand. There are more impressionable, movable votes within reach in both an actual and relative sense than for a number of decades. The main part could go right, left, turn off, swing erratically, divide inconclusively, or become a personal following. But it will almost surely be felt, positively or negatively.[16]

To found a political movement solely in malaise and discontent is to build a house of cards. But the time may at last be right for candidates who share the late Adlai Stevenson's determination to "talk sense to the American people."

The Administration's problems with Watergate add up to a second reason for expecting considerable changes in Congress in 1974. The party in power tends normally to lose seats in an off-year election. The absence of a winning President's coattail's leaves some Administration supporters in a highly vulnerable position; and no President in history has ever been able to get quite as excited about campaigning for his party (in off-years) as about campaigning for himself.

More than that, administrations make enemies. Anthony Downs called this the "coalition of minorities" problem, where an administration could act with majority support on each issue yet gradually dissatisfy enough minorities to insure its defeat.[17] In almost every recent case, presidential popularity has shown "a general downward trend as he is forced on a variety of issues to act and thus create intense, unforgiving opponents of former supporters."[18] Republican congressmen will have difficulty escaping Nixon's enemies. Ironically, it doesn't seem to matter how congressmen of the President's party vote. The 1958 farm revolt against the Eisenhower-Benson policy of low supports, for example, hurt Republican farm-belt representatives regardless of their personal stands on the issue.[19] Democratic incumbents do not have the advantages which an incumbent administration can provide, but they don't have to carry its excess baggage either. For members of both parties, then, the combination of Watergate and minority coalitions founded in such problems as inflation, unemployment, racial tension and cutbacks in housing, health, and education funds is likely to lead to a campaign strategy stressing independence from the Administration.

A third important factor in off-year elections is low voter turnout. Low turnout, as pointed out, tends to favor the status quo. Massive volunteer efforts, however, can reverse this trend. One effect of door-to-door canvassing, as we shall see in later chapters, is to increase turnout. Thus, in an off-year selective canvassing activities—aimed only at neighborhoods with a high potential for supporting your candidate —are less likely to be offset by other, opposing, appeals.

A district that in 1972 elected a Democrat by a margin of 85,000 to 75,000 might be expected to re-elect him in 1974 by a margin of 58,000 to 50,000. The percentages remain the same; but the number of added voters needed by a Republican challenger is diminished to 8,000 from 10,000. With this size voter turnout he has, moreover, a probable reservoir of 25,000 stay-at-homes from whom—if they can be identified—to draw upon for those needed votes. Because turnout in off-year primaries is even lower than in general elections, the possibility of "stealing" an election through selective canvassing is even greater. Thus in the 1970 elections, only seventeen House incumbents were defeated, but nine—more than half—bit the dust in primaries.

The final reason for anticipating the election of a new Congress in 1974 is partisan. The Democrats should be the big gainers. The natural tendency of the party in power in the White House to lose seats in an off-year will be compounded in 1974 by a second characteristic of the off-year electorate: its tendency to vote party. A 1958 poll by the Survey Research Center of the University of Michigan showed that an "astonishingly small proportion of the midterm vote is cast by political independents," and it was the independent vote that elected Nixon. Moreover, "something like 84 per cent of all the votes for the House in 1958 were cast by party identifiers supporting their parties."[20] Although the percentage identifying themselves with neither major party has increased substantially since 1958, 76 per cent of those voting in 1970 were party-identifiers casting party-line votes.[21] Democrats, moreover, still maintain an overwhelming advantage over Republicans in the percentage of party-identifiers.

We are not suggesting that the Democratic party has a monopoly on virtue. But the tendency for Democrats to be somewhat more progressive in outlook and thus somewhat more open to concepts of change and reform is compounded—in the short run, at least—by the dynamics of divided government. In the words of David Truman:

> The imperatives of Presidential politics produce more than an echo in the congressional party, and the partisan responses at either end of Pennsylvania Avenue have a detectable mutual resemblance.[21]

This "mutual resemblance" has manifested itself in recent years on a number of key issues. Because he is their President, many Republicans have felt compelled to uphold Nixon vetoes on environment, health, and education programs that they otherwise would have supported. Similarly, they have defended, though often with strong reservations, presidential prerogatives in the impounding of funds, in foreign policy, and in the withholding of information from Congress. Democratic assertions of legislative authority, conversely, are not unblemished by opportunistic, partisan motivations. Many of President Johnson's most automatic supporters became overnight doves when the war in Southeast Asia became Nixon's rather than Johnson's responsibility. And many of the problems that Congress now confronts can be traced back to the enthusiastic determination of Democratic congresses to give "their" Presidents, Johnson and Kennedy, anything they wanted in the form of new powers. In the long run, then, there is no guarantee that Democratic victories in 1974 will result in a revitalized Congress. But as John Maynard Keynes once said, in the long run we're all dead; for now, at least, victory for the Democrats is likely to mean a strengthening of the legislative branch.

What the prospects for change ultimately depend upon, however, are the decisions of reform-minded citizens on whether or not to become involved. In 1970 the invasion of Cambodia and the killings at Kent State galvanized large groups of volunteers into action. The question of whether or not our system of legislative democracy can survive, though vitally important, does not have the instant dramatic appeal of those 1970 issues. If the end of the Vietnam war has meant the end of the peace movement, if students have to be killed in order for the electorate to be activated, then the prospects for meaningful legislative change are slim indeed.

THE HARD REALITIES OF
EFFECTIVE ACTION

Winning elections is more than just hard work. Success in politics requires skill, dedication, and a *willingness to work with what you've got.*

No one has ever been able scientifically to identify the forces that combine to produce a successful politician. Why was Dwight Eisenhower a winner and Adlai Stevenson a loser? What strange combination of circumstances elevated the nationally unknown Spiro Agnew to his lofty post in our system? These are fascinating questions for a seminar in American government, but they can be deadly traps for the amateur politician. The fact is that for most of us, most of the time, we must work with what we have in terms of candidates.

This is not due to any conscious conspiracy. Amateur activists are by definition part-time politicians whose political calendars are governed by elections. In most districts, however, the process of candidate recruitment must begin long before. In a state with a June primary, for example, the deadline for filing petitions usually falls in early April. The touching of bases, the building of an organization, the establishment of contacts throughout the district must begin, then, long before the spring leaves are on the trees.

And who are you going to get to run? To begin with, the assumption that there is a large reservoir of electable individuals just waiting to be asked simply does not hold up. Despite its attractive features, being a congressman is a hard job. It involves quitting one's (often more lucrative) job, moving to Washington, and being on call seven days a week—features that might not be too attractive to a mother or a family man or to someone who likes his present occupation and income. But if being a congressman is hard, being a candidate is worse. An effective campaign goes seven days a week *and* twenty-odd hours a day. It can begin at 6 A.M. at the factory gates and continue to midnight or later in party clubhouses, union halls, and bars. Foot sores from walking, finger blisters from shaking hands, cheeks sore from too much smiling, and ulcers from endless cups of bilious coffee are traditional occupational hazards of a political candidate.

Campaign volunteers have to learn that those who are most

willing to run for office are not necessarily best qualified, and you can't beat somebody with nobody. General prominence helps, but it is not a guarantee of campaign appeal. As in horse racing, a track record helps. More than four in five members of Congress in 1972 had previously served in other elective offices. Finally, it is important to remember that a congressional district embraces nearly 500,000 people: the hero of Podunk may be unknown in Mudville, and vice versa. We will have more to say on candidate recruitment in Chapter 4. The point here is simply that we normally have to place our bets on the horses that are already on the track.

The situation for change, however, is not all that hopeless. Although the parties on a national basis often seem rather much alike, in any given state or congressional district the differences are likely to be quite significant. It is important in evaluating candidates not to be completely taken in by political labels. Or by appearances—some unappealing men in Congress vote right and some very appealing men in Congress vote wrong. Here, then, is Rule 2 of practical politics: *Keep your eye upon the doughnut and not upon the hole*. Remember that there is no perfect candidate, no Lochinvar on a white steed who has the perfect solution to each and every one of the problems confronting us. But the differences between candidates are usually differences that are worth fighting about.

One more word on political effectiveness. It is surprising how many otherwise rational voters voluntarily renounce their right to participate in the process of picking candidates. There is nothing wrong with thinking of yourself as an independent, but unless your state has an open primary it is foolish to register as one. As Frederik Pohl puts it:

> The man who values his independent judgment too much to submit to the dictates of a political party has put himself in a position where he can do nothing *but* submit to the dictates of a political party. When the basic de-

cisions were made, he was home telling his wife what a principled man he was. . . .

If you really want to have anything to say about who runs your government, you not only have to vote, you have to vote often. You have to vote in many different kinds of elections. Above all you have to vote in the primaries.[22]

Registering for a party to vote in its primary in no way alters your right to split your ticket, to vote for the opposition, or to stay home in November. Keeping your eye on the "doughnut" means voting in primaries even if you sully your independent skirts in doing so. What is more important, your purity or the nation's?

Almost of necessity, politics in a representative democracy involves "lesser evilism." In a system of majority rule, winning is the name of the game. To win, a candidate must appeal not just to you but to 40,000 to 100,000 other voters. The composition of the district may therefore dictate a campaign based on economic issues rather than on ecology. It may call for emphasizing a very narrow set of local issues, such as help for the fishing industry or opposition to government plans to close down a veterans' hospital. If issues such as these can win votes for your candidate, these are the issues that should be pushed. As campaign consultant Matthew A. Reese says, "To win, you don't talk with a guy who has lost his job about the development of the foreign policy which led to Vietnam—even if, by chance, you understand it. . . . Fit the issue to the voter."

Simple as this sounds, it is difficult in practice. Most of us will work in the 1974 campaign because we feel very strongly about certain issues. But those who want to be active in politics so they can talk about boycotting grapes can throw this book away. That is not what political campaigns are all about. Stephen Shadegg, who engineered Barry Goldwater's (R., Arizona) initial upset campaign for the Senate, argues:

Voters don't elect philosophers to public office, they elect candidates. Approached in the right fashion at the right time, a voter can be persuaded to give his ballot to a candidate whose philosophy is opposed to the cherished notions of the voter.[23]

Perhaps this is too cynical and hard-nosed. It may also be true. Keeping your eye upon the doughnut means remembering at all times that one new vote in Congress for principles in which you believe is worth far more than one or two browbeaten converts in a door-to-door campaign. Again the basic point: *Election boards count votes, not issues.*

ELECTIONS ARE WON AT THE MARGINS

Counting both House and Senate, there will be 470 congressional elections in 1974. Close to 1,000 major-party candidates for federal office will be seeking volunteer campaign help. Another 8,000 to 10,000 candidates for state and local office will be on the prowl for live bodies. Most of them will get far less than they need. Many will get more than they deserve.

Given limited resources, effective political action must be selective political action. Thus Rule 3: *When you're hunting ducks, you go where the ducks are.* Similarly, when your goal is the election of a new Congress, you go where you have a reasonable chance of winning. In Appendix A we have listed the nation's ninety-nine most marginal congressional districts; these are the districts for us to focus attention on this fall. The choice, as Matthew Reese puts it, is between enjoying "the excitement and publicity of reducing the victory margin of a hawk you cannot possibly beat" or using "the same manpower and time to elect several peace candidates in less glamorous marginal districts."

Between 1952 and 1968, 785 seats in the House of Representatives (20.1 per cent) were won by candidates who received less than 55 per cent of the two-party vote. Of those who ran again in the following election, 125 (17.5 per cent) were defeated. Of the more than 3,000 incumbents who had received more than 55 per cent of the vote, only 4.5 per cent were defeated in the next election. Not a single one of the candidates receiving more than 65 per cent of the two-party vote in 1966 were defeated in 1968.

It is highly unlikely that many upsets of incumbents will be scored this year either. To some voters, the prospect of working to put certain entrenched incumbents out to pasture is too juicy to pass up. And it might be fun to work in the campaigns of certain well-established and well-known long-term members. Forget it. Remember the ducks. It would probably be more comfortable to hunt ducks from your front porch, but if you are serious about victory you avoid both the hopeless cause and the sure thing. Enthusiasm is not enough. To win, you must carefully focus and direct your resources.

Lyndon Johnson once said that there were only three things that concerned the average voter: "Everybody worries about war and peace. The men worry about heart attacks and the women worry about cancer of the tit."[24] The analysis, if somewhat crudely put, comes uncomfortably close to the mark. There is simply no way that you are going to arouse some people to register and vote. No way that you persuade others to change their minds. This is why, above all, the chances of turning around a district that is more than six to four against you at the outset are very remote.

What should the campaign activist do, then, in those 300 or more congressional districts that are virtually safe in 1974 for one party or the other? Move? Work for a candidate for some other office? A Senate race sometimes offers more realistic possibilities, and contests for state and local offices can also be important. Another alternative is to focus on a primary challenge. The good thing about the primary route is that it bypasses the built-in party vote advantage that makes the district safe to begin with. The bad thing, however, is that the incumbent enjoys tremendous advantages in primary campaigns; he is likely to have the support of party organizations, access to funds, and, most significantly, a pattern of name-recognition that few challengers can match. The Survey Research Center's 1958 study showed, for example, that

> Of the people who lived in districts where the House seat was contested in 1958, 59%—well over half—said that they had neither read nor heard anything about either candidate for Congress, and less than one in five felt that they knew something about both candidates.

But the incumbents enjoyed a special advantage:

> In districts where an incumbent was opposed for reelection in 1958, 39% of our respondents knew something about the Congressman, whereas only 20% said they knew anything about his nonincumbent opponent.[25]

This latter advantage is particularly difficult to overcome in a primary campaign. Thus the primary route is likely to be successful only when the challenger is well-known in his or her own right, has adequate financing, and is blessed by luck.

Sometimes a losing battle is worth the fight. Certainly it is more important to engage in an occasional losing cause than it is to back a sure thing. In the words of Lawrence of Arabia: "There could be no honour in sure success but much might be wrested from a sure defeat." The challenger who takes a long view of the campaign can use defeat to build a constituency and organization for the future. By successively narrowing the margins, it is sometimes possible to turn a once-safe district around. For example, John Brademas (D., Indiana), today the deputy whip in the House, lost twice—in 1954 and 1956—before finally winning in the Democratic landslide of 1958. But constituency-building is a hard job. Not only are few people willing to work at politics year round, but the two-year cycle of congressional elections has

a tendency to dull memories and make it difficult for the
loser to sustain any forward momentum. A defeated candidate, moreover, is no longer good copy for the press and will
find it increasingly difficult and frustrating to compete with
the incumbent for media attention.

A losing campaign can also be effective in calling attention to new issues or arousing incumbents into a an aware-
ness of new constituencies. A well-organized single-issue campaign can, at the least, force the incumbent to come to grips
with that issue. At best, it can even turn him around. This
is particularly true during periods of political uncertainty.
When President Nixon sent troops into Cambodia in 1970,
Congressman Edward J. Patten (D., New Jersey) concluded
"after a long and sleepless night" that he would have to support the President's decision. Two days later the Movement
for a New Congress sent 200 student volunteers into Middle-
sex County to work for Patten's primary opponent, Lew
Kaden. The next day Patten reconsidered his stand and ac-
cused Nixon of a "tragic blunder in sending American soldiers
to Cambodia." Such moral victories for reformers are not
common, but they help to sweeten the bitter pill of defeat.

One final possibility a volunteer would find worth exploring
is the state legislatures. Surely these are among the sickest of
American political institutions. The typical state legislature,
Willie Morris once wrote,

> is a fertile source for a writer. So many crimes are com-
> mitted there daily in an atmosphere of a service club
> social, and the human flaws are so accessible. Sometimes
> it is too much for one to bear the more or less constant
> spectacle of legislatures backed by the sanction of power-
> ful business lobbies frustrating the few good and intel-
> ligent men who are willing to labor in the maw of small-
> time politics.[26]

State legislatures are important in their own right and
deserve far more serious citizen attention than they have re-

ceived. They also have an important effect on national politics. By drawing election district lines and by writing the major laws relating to voter registration, elections, and political parties, their impact on congressional elections is significant. And by providing campaign experience and public visibility, a seat in the state legislature provides a good starting point for a congressional career.

WHAT YOU CAN DO TO MAKE CONGRESS MORE EFFECTIVE

Right now, the major battleground for control of America's future is Congress. "Legislative reassertion," as Louis Fisher warns, "is not in itself . . . a fool-proof antidote for future Vietnams and large defense budgets." It is, however, the best hope we have for the survival of a system of representative government. The battle between the President and Congress is not a zero-sum game in which the reinvigoration of one means the diminution of the other. The President alone cannot control the bureaucracy; even his own personal staff— as the Watergate affair tragically illustrates—may be beyond his command. If Congress is flawed, "neither is there hope in legislative acquiescence to 'executive expertise' especially when the latter becomes a synonym for incompetence and deceit." Thus,

> There must be a new temperament and attitude among legislators: a courage to resist being stampeded into granting power simply because the President waves the flag; a resolve to defer to no one in the exercise of independent judgment; a determination to treat "reassertion" not as a temporary phenomenon—needed to restore constitutional balance—but as a permanent, non-delegable legislative responsibility. Congress has demonstrated rather impressively that it can change its attitudes and its procedures and contribute intelligently to foreign policy-making. The larger question is whether it has the

will and the staying power to contribute from one year to the next, in times of crisis as well as relative calm, without reverting to its habitual acquiescence to the President.[27]

Whether or not Congress demonstrates such staying power depends upon whether or not the public encourages it to do so. And the major burden of responsibility falls on what Yale University political scientist Robert Dahl calls "the political strata," those who know the most about politics and who are most able and willing to act politically. Ignorance of Congress is an enduring characteristic of the American people. Indeed it is this massive public ignorance which most distinguishes congressional campaigns from presidential ones. And it is this "ignorance gap" which has allowed Congress to delegate and dissipate its constitutional role.

Paradoxically, this "ignorance gap" also provides unusual openings for activists. The statistics which show that most voters cannot even identify their congressmen by name are depressing from the perspective of democratic theory; but they can be very comforting to the candidate who is able to mobilize masses of volunteer campaigners. Resistant as most typically apolitical citizens are to billboards, broadsides, and the media, they can hardly ignore the message of a personal visit. From their point of view, you are the campaign.

Another factor makes House and Senate races more vulnerable to volunteer efforts: the relative lack of concern for Congress generally expressed by regular party organizations. In the words of former Senator Clark, "concern for the Presidency in national elections and concern with state and local offices, particularly executive offices with their attendant patronage and fund-raising perquisites, come close to exhausting the attention of the regular party organization." Clark learned his lesson the hard way from a party stalwart who bluntly told him: "Never mind all that stuff that goes on in Washington. What about jobs in the Highway Department?"

The point is simply that for those who are interested in "all that stuff that goes on in Washington," the field is open. It is open in particular to those who remember the *three basic rules of volunteer activism:*

1. Don't be easily discouraged.
2. Keep your eye upon the doughnut and not upon the hole. Make victory your goal.
3. Focus energy by hunting where the ducks are.

Victory in November is not enough. Effective political action requires follow-through. Being a congressman is a hard job: one can put in a very full week by simply answering the mail, entertaining constituents, performing routine services, and occasionally wandering over to the floor of the House for a vote or quorum call. "This life," one congressman told a Brookings Institute roundtable, "consists of preoccupation with the unimportant at the expense of the more important."[28] As long as it remains true "that you are re-elected or defeated on the basis of what you do in the office rather than what you do on the floor,"[29] this will remain the case and Congress will remain weak.

Whether or not it remains true depends essentially on what the political strata demand. The American political system is amazingly vulnerable to the machinations of dedicated minorities. That these minorities have been more often devoted to the advancement of private rather than public interests is both an indicator and a cause of the current crisis. It is in your power to reverse this imbalance.

ACTIVISM OFFERS SOME PERSONAL
   DIVIDENDS

The old phrase "politics makes strange bedfellows" is not meant to suggest that working in a political campaign is analogous to joining a club of sexual swingers. That happens, but the far more frequent social reward is the opportunity that campaign activity brings for contact with a diverse group of people. More, probably, than any other organizational umbrella, a political campaign covers an amazingly broad spectrum of social, economic, and political classes. For the curious and the tolerant there are few better opportunities to meet new people and to expand social horizons.

For those with secret or overt political ambitions of their own, there is nothing like starting at the bottom where you can learn through trial and error at someone else's expense. And for those who are simply curious about the way things work, there is no better way to start learning than by talking with voters and by participating in the day-to-day activities of the "real thing."

Politics is a deadly serious game that is fun. Even the losses get some rewards. Citizen power in a democracy is located in the ballot box. Whether your candidate wins or loses, you can help decide the future of American politics. Campaign activity provides as good an opportunity as our system allows to encourage meaningful dialogue between citizens of differing points of view. It stands as the single most effective form of lobbying yet devised. It is the best possible counter to the distorting effects of big money in political campaigns. And it is the breeding ground for long-range change: in 1974's grass-roots volunteer efforts, the results of the 1976 presidential and congressional campaigns and the directions of change in our system as a whole will be cultivated and shaped.

NOTES

1. Henry Steele Commager, "The Misuse of Power," *The New Republic,* April 17, 1971.

2. Duane Lockard, *The Perverted Priorities of American Politics* (New York: Macmillan, 1971), p. 242.

3. Stuart Symington, "Congress's Right to Know," *New York Times Magazine*, August 9, 1970.

4. Kenneth Bradshaw and David Pring, *Parliament and Congress* (Austin, Tex.: University of Texas Press, 1972), pp. 365–66.

5. Reprinted by Senator Frank Church in the *Congressional Record* (January 18, 1973), 93rd Congress, First Session, p. 971.

6. Allen Schick, "An Analysis of Proposals to Improve Congressional Control of Spending," in United States Senate Committee on Government Operations, Subcommittee on Budgeting, Management and Expenditures, *Improving Congressional Control over the Budget: A Compendium of Materials* (Washington, D.C.: Government Printing Office, 1973), p. 217.

7. *Congressional Quarterly Weekly Report*, January 23, 1973, p. 119.

8. Aaron Wildavsky, "The Annual Expenditure Increment," in United States Senate Committee on Government Operations, Subcommittee on Budgeting, Management and Expenditures, *Improving Congressional Control over the Budget: Hearings* (Washington, D.C.: Government Printing Office, 1973), p. 494.

9. From President Nixon's January 1973 Budget Message, quoted in *Hearings Before the Ad Hoc Subcommittee on Impoundment of Funds*, United States Senate, 93rd Congress, 1st Session, p. 270.

10. Elliot Richardson, ibid., p. 298.

11. Lewis A. Froman, *Congressmen and Their Constituencies* (Chicago: Rand-McNally, 1963), p. 80.

12. William Riordan, *Plunkitt of Tammany Hall* (New York: Dutton, 1963), p. 51.

13. Quoted in Charles Clapp, *The Congressman* (Garden City, N.Y.: Doubleday Anchor, 1964), p. 58.

14. Joseph S. Clark, *The Sapless Branch* (New York: Harper & Row, 1965), pp. 76–77.
15. Michael Walzer, *Political Action: A Practical Guide to Movement Politics* (Chicago: Quadrangle Books, 1971), p. 18.
16. Frederick G. Dutton, *Changing Sources of Power* (New York: McGraw-Hill, 1971), pp. xiii, 25.
17. Anthony Downs, *An Economic Theory of Democracy* (New York: Harper & Row, 1957), pp. 55–60.
18. John E. Mueller, "Presidential Popularity from Truman to Johnson," *American Political Science Review*, 64 (March 1970), p. 20.
19. Thomas V. Gilpatrick, "Price Support Policy and the Midwest Farm Vote," *Midwest Journal of Political Science*, 3 (November 1959), pp. 319–35.
20. Donald E. Stokes and Warren E. Miller, "Party Government and the Saliency of Congress," in Angus Campbell, et. al., *Elections and the Political Order* (New York: Wiley, 1966), pp. 197–98.
21. David B. Truman, *The Congressional Party* (New York: Wiley, 1959), p. 300.
22. Frederik Pohl, *Practical Politics 1972* (New York: Ballantine Books, 1971), p. 10.
23. Stephen Shadegg, *The New How to Win an Election* (New York: Taplinger, 1964), p. 10.
24. Quoted in David Halberstam, *The Best and the Brightest* (New York: Random House, 1972), p. 423.
25. Stokes and Miller, op. cit., p. 204.
26. Willie Morris, "Legislating in Texas," *Commentary*, November 1964, p. 37.
27. Louis Fisher, *President and Congress* (New York: Free Press, 1972), pp. 234–35.
28. Quoted in Clapp, op. cit., p. 58.
29. Ibid., p. 59.

CHAPTER 2

POWER IN CONGRESS

Of our major institutions, Congress is probably the least loved. For political columnists and editorial writers Congress is always a convenient whipping boy when a story is needed. Political cartoonists have almost as much fun with "Senator Claghorn" caricatures as they do with Richard Nixon's nose and jowls. Unfortunately, Congress and the men and women who make it up all too often provide ample ammunition for their critics by unwise, intemperate, and occasionally illegal actions.

Congress is also probably our least understood institution. Theoretically the branch of government closest to the people, it is seen by many Americans as Byzantinely complex, too distantly removed from their own concerns, or simply "irrelevant." During the 1950s and 1960s political scientists and political pundits argued that the presidency was the repository of all virtue and the embodiment of the public will. The example of the last two Presidents progressively insulating themselves from the people and persisting in policies opposed by a majority of Americans has shattered that view of the presidency. The Watergate hearings and the numerous other executive-congressional confrontations have fo-

cused the public's attention on Capitol Hill for the first time
in a long while. In Chapter 1 we discussed congressional elections. Many readers have been or will be active in congressional campaigns. But what goes on after your candidate gets
there? How important and effective will he be when he has to
change roles from candidate to legislator? How successful will
he be in realizing the policy aims of his election platform?
The answers to these and similar questions can only be gotten
by understanding the milieu in which he will have to operate
after he is elected, as well as the other players with whom
he must compete and co-operate. In this chapter we will
attempt to give a quick view of the internal workings and
power relationships of Congress.

CONGRESS AS AN INSTITUTION:
The Little World of Capitol Hill

In many respects Congress may be best visualized as a
club. We are not thinking of William S. White's characteriza-
tion of the 1950s Senate as an "inner club"[1] of power and
privilege.[2] Rather, Congress is more like a private club in its
ambiance and its behavioral norms, with its leather tufted
chairs and heavy velvet draperies, its private gymnasiums
and anterooms. Along the railing which rings the House floor
there is an inordinate amount of backslapping and story
swapping. Elaborate routines of courtesy and deference
dominate even the most divisive debates. Certain types of
people are able to adjust to and function in an atmosphere
like this better than others. In part, it is a matter of personality and temperament. Dour ideologues who don't enjoy
spending a moment bantering with a colleague probably will
not fare well.

Learning and understanding the formal rules of Congress
are important for any member who wants to become an
effective legislator.[3] But of equal importance are the informal

rules—the norms of expected behavior that arise in any group that has extensive, sustained face-to-face interaction.[4]

Probably the most important informal rule among congressmen as among almost all politicians is "keeping your word." Some people find it amusing to hear a politician say that "his word is his bond." Yet it really shouldn't be so surprising. Much of politics consists of various kinds of bargains and compromises. A very common type of bargain is the "logroll." In other words, Congressman Wheat agrees to vote for the cotton bill if Congressman Cotton votes for the wheat bill. Most logrolls are not simultaneous but rather involve a promise of some future action. A congressman who fails to live up to his end of the bargain after getting what he wanted is a member with whom most legislators will be chary to bargain. Moreover, since the terms of many logrolls are implicit rather than explicit, the necessity for having a reputation as a fair dealer is even more important.

For a long time, a new member was expected to be seen but not heard. He was expected to learn the formal and informal rules and work hard on his or her committees and subcommittees. His maiden speech was not expected until his second year and even then it was expected to be limited to a specialized area of concern to the freshman's committee or constituency. This norm, while still operative, has been declining in recent years as more and more freshmen have begun playing an active role on the floor in their first year.[5]

Like any institution Congress rewards hard work. A shared feeling of being hard workers is one of the major integrating norms on the prestigious House Appropriations Committee,[6] but it is a norm that applies almost as strongly to the House as a whole. All congressmen have two constituencies—the people in their districts and their fellow members. A member who plays to the galleries and newspapers at home to the detriment of his relationships with his colleagues in Washington sacrifices internal effectiveness and power. In the early sixties, nothing galled House Foreign Affairs Committee members more than to turn on the evening news and see their fellow member John V. Lindsay (R., New York) holding an impromptu press conference on the Capitol steps while they had been working all day (often until midnight), without the benefit of his presence, on the foreign aid bill.

Especially in the House, with its much larger membership, it is necessary for a member to specialize in one or two policy areas if he is to wield any internal influence. Specialization, which is a necessary norm in any "modern" organization of substantial size, allows for a rational division of the work load and, most importantly, gives the Congress a means of acquiring the expertise and information necessary for it to compete with the Executive. However, specialization combined with Congress' structural characteristic of a decentralization of power has led to a situation where it is almost impossible to co-ordinate authorizations and appropriations or to consider the trade-offs of various courses of action.

Another important norm is reciprocity. The late Speaker Sam Rayburn (D., Texas) used to tell new House members that "to get along, go along." Given our type of political system with its nonideological character and low degree of party cohesion, the various competing factions and interests would often end up in stalemate without such a norm.

Bargaining and compromise are basic parts of our political system, yet they are often tainted words. Much of the public's mistrust of politics derives from American civics training which holds up a model of politics derived from a nonempirical, heavily normative democratic theory that emphasizes the importance and centrality of individual action. But it also derives from a basic misunderstanding of the nature of congressional politics.

Two important characteristics of that politics are "first, that imperfect agreement exists upon the goals to be realized and, second, that resources for influencing these goals are widely distributed among the actors."[7] The table below depicts the kinds of relationships that result from the various combinations of these two variables.

Table II

Types of Political Relationships

Resources	Goals	
	SHARED	UNSHARED
Equal	Problem solving	Bargaining
Unequal	Leadership persuasion	Command

SOURCE: Roger Davidson, *The Role of the Congressman* (New York: Pegasus, 1969), p. 24.

When any group of players agrees on goals and their resources are equal, they merely have to devise the best means of realizing their goals. When goals are unshared and resources are unequal, those in a superior position must coerce their subordinates to act. Neither of these relationships are often present in real life in anything approaching their pure form. The agreement on goals of problem solving often disappears when means of achieving those goals are discussed. And even in an army, many command situations are marked by a great deal of persuasion and even implicit bargaining.

Richard Neustadt has emphasized the persuasive aspect of presidential leadership. He observes that "the essence of a President's persuasive task with congressmen and everybody else, is to induce them to believe that what he wants of them is what their own appraisal of their own responsibilities require them to do in their interest, not his."[8] Lyndon Johnson operated in a similar manner as Senate Democratic leader in the 1950s. On any given bill his object was to put together a coalition of a majority of senators needed for passage. To that end he would try to structure the situation to make it as easy as possible for a majority of senators to see that their own interests would be served by going along with him.

The most important relationship is bargaining. This is the quintessential political relationship deriving from equal resources and different policy goals. The relative equality of members is caused by two factors. First, all members have one vote. Second, and more importantly, all members are ultimately responsible only to their constituencies for their continued tenure in Congress; party leaders in Congress cannot deny renomination to maverick members. Given this situation, a solution can be reached over differing policy goals only by bargaining and compromise.

The refusal to bargain can only lead to a stalemate. It has been this aspect of the behavior of many liberals and hard-line conservatives that has caused them to be considerably less effective than they might. Former Senator Paul Douglas (D., Illinois) introduced a number of innovative and needed pieces of legislation during his eighteen years in the Senate. However, his reluctance to compromise —to take half a loaf instead of none—resulted in few of these bills actually getting passed. Most of Douglas' legislative initiatives were later shepherded through Congress by similarly progressive but considerably more flexible members.

A number of other liberals besides Douglas have adopted the "outsiders' role." While this role may be more personally satisfying to the individual, in that it allows him to speak out on a wide range of issues, it also makes him a less effective legislator. In his classic study of the outsider's role, Ralph Huitt comments that "the behavior associated with the Outsider may be functional for protest groups seeking a spokesman, dysfunctional for groups needing leverage inside the legislative body"[9] and it can be used in particular to call attention to neglected problems; but it seldom produces new laws.

Important decisions affecting the lives of millions of Americans are made daily within the halls of Congress. Members who adopt the outsider role do so at the cost of relinquishing influence on these decisions. Unfortunately, those from highly competitive districts often feel that they must adopt the outsider's role in order to survive politically. Nicholas Masters has described "responsible" legislators—those, in other words, with the greatest influence—as men who

> serve to enhance the prestige and importance of the body . . . have respect for the legislative process . . . understand and appreciate its formal and informal rules . . . have the respect of their fellows . . . don't try to manipulate every situation for personal advantage . . . are willing to compromise . . . have a moderate approach.[10]

In an analysis of why Carl Albert, the present House Speaker, defeated the more externally well-known Richard W. Bolling (D., Missouri) for majority leader in 1962, observers repeatedly referred to Albert's role style. One interviewee described Albert's approach to his job:

> [he] developed quite a genius for knowing what people would do . . . Another service he performed endears him to people. Carl's the kind of guy everybody could find.[11]

In order to "know what people would do" and be a "guy everybody could find," members must spend inordinate amounts of time in the often dreary job of staying on the floor instead of attending to the mass of other business most Congressmen have. Albert prided himself in spending a greater proportion of his time on the floor of the House than any other member did and was continually accessible to his colleagues. Sticking to internal legislative business and eschewing speech making, publicity tours, and so on is the

way such men get the feel for the House's mores and temperament that is essential to an effective legislative leader.

The differing styles of Senators Robert F. Kennedy (D.,
New York) and Edward M. Kennedy (D., Massachusetts)
offer a good example of contrasting role behavior. Robert
Kennedy failed to observe the usual apprenticeship period
for freshman senators and was continually speaking out on
the principal issues of the day. He also was frequently absent
and did little to cultivate internal influence in the Senate.
On the other hand, his younger brother in his early years
in the Senate went along with the Senate's folkways. He
waited the expected time before making a major speech.
At the end of the day, he often dropped in on his chairman
on the Judiciary Committee, James O. Eastland (D., Mississippi), to share a bourbon and branch water and discuss
the day's legislative happenings. Such assiduous cultivation
of the Senate's mores paid off when Edward Kennedy was
able to defeat a member of the Senate's establishment,
Russell B. Long (D., Louisiana), for the majority whip position in 1969. Former Senator Wayne L. Morse (D., Oregon),
himself a prototypical outsider, attributed Kennedy's victory
to the undisputed feeling in the Senate that he was a hard-
working senator who had a strong allegiance to the Senate as
a body and respected its rules and traditions.

The post-Chappaquiddick Ted Kennedy paid less and less
attention to his Senate duties. As a result, he was defeated
for party whip in 1971 by the much less well-known Robert
C. Byrd (D., West Virginia). As Secretary of the Democratic Conference, Byrd had taken care of much of the day-
to-day Senate business for Majority Leader Mike Mansfield
as well as carrying out many of the duties of the Senate
whips he served with, Russell Long and Edward Kennedy.
His stunning defeat of Kennedy was typical of Byrd's
methodical approach to Senate politics. He did not announce
his candidacy until he was certain that he had a one-vote

majority. Byrd got the winning vote by proxy from a dying Senator Richard B. Russell (D., Georgia). Although few people outside West Virginia knew Robert Byrd, he had established himself as a major power in the Senate by his elaborate attention to detail and his cordial relations with a number of senators for whom he had done favors. Former Senator Eugene J. McCarthy (D., Minnesota) tells an apt anecdote about the time early in a session when he asked Byrd to let him know when a certain piece of legislation in which McCarthy was interested would reach the floor. Almost nine months later McCarthy was taken aback when Byrd tapped him on the shoulder to tell him "that bill you were interested in will be coming out of Judiciary this week." McCarthy was ashamed to admit that he could not recall what Byrd was talking about. But out of such assiduous cultivation of other members' interests and devotion to detail and hard work comes internal influence in Congress.

Why do so many liberals adopt the outsider role? Ideology is part of the answer: since congressional norms tend to have a conservative bias favoring the status quo, it is the liberal who is out of step. Temperament is also a factor: those who wish to change the system can be easily discouraged by the slow pace of the legislative process. In many cases, however, liberals are ineffective because their constituents make it impossible not to be. Ironically, although liberals often have some of the most sophisticated constituents, they often reward their congressmen and senators for statements and behaviors that effectively cut them off from any real internal influence, thus reducing their ability to affect the nation's problems in anything but a symbolic way.

Statements in the House by Ronald V. Dellums (D., California) on the race problem in America, Bella Abzug on women's rights, or Shirley Chisholm on both undoubtedly serve an important function in bringing critical issues before the American public, but their ability to deal with these problems in an instrumental way is greatly reduced by their rejection of the insider role.

CONGRESSIONAL LEADERSHIP:
Elected Leaders and Feudal Barons

Modern leadership theory has had two major concerns. The first concern has been who becomes a leader and how. The second has been how do individuals become effective leaders? Congress, unlike the Executive, does not have *one* leader. While the Speaker is the ultimate leader of the House and the Majority Leader the *de facto* leader of the Senate, most observers would characterize the leadership structures of both bodies as collegial rather than hierarchical. Even more important, the leaders elected by the respective party members must share their power with another set of leaders —the committee and subcommittee chairmen—whose powers are relatively autonomous.

1. Formal Leaders

Appendix B lists the elected leadership positions in the House and the Senate and their occupants in the 93rd Congress. The duties of the highest offices of the Senate are mainly ceremonial. The President of the Senate is the Vice President. As presiding officer he has little political influence except in those rare instances when the Senate is deadlocked and he is able to cast the decisive vote. His most important function in this role is serving as a liaison between the President and the Senate. There has, however, been a great deal of variation in the attitudes of Vice Presidents toward their Senate role. Former Vice President Agnew, for example, showed little interest in presiding and was seldom seen on Capitol Hill.

Henry A. Wallace, President Franklin D. Roosevelt's third-term Vice President, did not command the respect of most Senators and had little rapport with them. On the other hand,

Vice Presidents who have been congressional leaders have played some important roles. In Roosevelt's first two terms "Cactus Jack" Garner, a former Speaker of the House, kept the President informed of congressional opinion as did former Senate Majority Leader Alben W. Barkley for President Truman. Former Senate Democratic leader Lyndon Johnson intended to stay actively involved in Senate affairs as Vice President, but toned his role down considerably when he realized that his interventions in Senate affairs were strongly resented.

The other ceremonial Senate office is the President Pro Tempore of the Senate, who presides in the absence of the Vice President. The Senator of the majority party with the greatest seniority, presently Senator Eastland, is appointed President Pro Tem, but he has little actual power.

The real party leaders of the Senate are the Majority and the Minority Leaders. Because he also holds several other important positions, due to party tradition the Democratic floor leader has considerably more power than his Republican counterpart. The Majority Leader, Mike Mansfield, is also Chairman of the Democratic Conference, the body comprising all Democratic senators which selects party leaders and serves as a forum for discussions of party strategy and legislative policy. He also chairs the Democratic Steering Committee, which makes committee assignments for Democrats, and the Policy Committee, which is responsible for scheduling Senate legislation. In addition, the Majority Leader appoints the chairman of the Senate Democrats' Campaign Committee which allocates contributions to the campaigns of Democratic senators. The Minority Leader, Hugh Scott, holds no such power; the Republicans fill each post with a different person.

Senators Byrd and Robert P. Griffin (R., Michigan) are the respective Democratic and Republican deputy leaders, or whips, whose duties and powers are roughly the same as those of their counterparts in the House, which are described below.

The Speaker of the House is the most important congressional leader. Besides being next in line after the Vice President in presidential succession, he is the presiding officer of the House and his party's leader there. The Speakership has developed and changed over the years since 1811 when Henry Clay was elected Speaker as a young first-term congressman out of the woods of Kentucky. Clay first came to power as a leader of the "war-hawks" faction in James Madison's administration and served intermittently as Speaker until 1825. The most important of the number of innovations he introduced into the office was to make the Speaker the leader of the majority party or faction in the House.

The importance of the Speaker declined during the next several decades preceding the Civil War. But in the post-Civil War era of congressional supremacy, the Speaker's office reassumed political significance.

A number of late nineteenth-century Speakers increased the powers and prestige of the position but the institutional and personal power of the Speaker reached its zenith under "Uncle Joe" Cannon (R., Illinois) who held the post from 1903 to 1910. This continual centralization of immense powers in the Speaker led to the "revolt of 1910–11" in which progressive Republicans, angered at Uncle Joe's dictatorial ways, deserted their party to join with the Democrats in selecting a new Speaker. In the process, the Speaker was stripped of his control over committee assignments and chairmanships, as well as losing his seat on the House Rules Committee.

While not as powerful as some pre-revolt Speakers, the present Speaker Carl Albert, still has a number of legislative powers. His power of recognition allows him to set the course and timing of debate. In cases where the jurisdiction of committees with regard to a particular piece of legislation is ambiguous, the Speaker decides which committee gets the bill. As unfriendly committees or committee chairmen can often kill a bill wanted by the leadership, bills are sometimes deliberately worded ambiguously in order to allow the Speaker to see that it goes to the most receptive committee. With the advice of the official House parliamentarian, Lewis Deschler, the Speaker rules on parliamentary procedure; in conjunction with the House Rules Committee, he schedules legislation. House members of Conference Committees are chosen by the Speaker. Speakers Rayburn and John W. McCormack (D., Massachusetts) informally influenced committee assignments—especially to the most important committees—and today both the Speaker and Majority Leader sit on the Democratic Committee on Committees which make House assignments.

The Speaker's most important resource, however, is positional. He is at the center of the House's communications network. He knows more about what's going on where and who wants what than any other member. And since in politics "information is power," he is more powerful than any other member.

The Speaker's second in command is the Majority Leader, presently Thomas P. O'Neill, Jr. (D., Massachusetts). The Majority Leader is the Speaker's man on the floor, playing an important role in scheduling legislation. He must also be willing to do the infighting in partisan battles for the Speaker who supposedly remains above the fray. McCormack, the Majority Leader under Speaker Rayburn for over twenty years, particularly relished going down into the well to engage in the biting give and take of legislative debate. When he succeeded Rayburn as Speaker upon the latter's death in 1962, he often found it difficult to restrain the old urges to take up the partisan battle again.

The losing candidate for Speaker, (the election for which is almost always along strict party lines), becomes the Minority Leader. Because a change in their respective party's electoral fortunes could result in their positions being reversed, the Speaker will usually allow the Minority Leader some input into scheduling and recognition. Like the Speaker, much of the Minority Leader's power derives from his central location in his party's communication network in the House.

His position as a leader of the *minority* party, however, creates some special problems for him. If the majority party in Congress also controls the White House, the minority party usually has to react to the majority's initiatives rather than advance a program of its own. The Minority Leader then often has to bolster the morale of his colleagues who continually find themselves on the losing side of the voting on the floor and are unable to exercise influence in their committees where the chairmen are always members of the majority party. This has become a serious problem in recent years for House Republicans, who have been able to capture a majority of House seats in only two elections in the last forty years. Several senior Republicans, believing they would never realize their dream of becoming chairmen of their committees, decided not to run for re-election in the last election.

Because Minority Leaders often become the lightning rods for fellow party members' frustrations over their minority status, they tend to retire or be overthrown more often than Majority Leaders.[12]

The party leaders sit atop an extensive communications network in the House—the principal agents of which are the party whips. Although the name "whips" has a disciplinary connotation, much of the whips' activities are concerned with transmitting information between the leadership and the rank-and-file members.

Randall Ripley has identified three other important functions the whips perform for the leadership in addition to information transmittal.[13] First, they try to ensure maximum attendance of party members at voting time through whip notices or calls to congressmen's offices to warn of impending legislation. They have been known to try to hold airplanes or change reservations so that a member would be able to cast his vote and still make a speaking commitment outside Washington. For members who cannot be present, they will attempt to arrange a "pair." Finally, they will often try to pressure wavering or uncommitted members to vote with the party leaders.

The present congressional Democratic leadership has not been as active as many had hoped. Speaker Albert and Senate Majority Leader Mansfield have failed to present a cohesive, alternative program to the Nixon administration's. They have met together to discuss legislation but they have not made a concentrated effort to co-ordinate their strategies and energies.

In terms of their leadership style, both men seem content to react to presidential initiatives and somewhat reluctant to bring all the resources of their positions to bear on fellow party members who do not follow the leadership's position. For many years Mansfield was a vocal critic of the war in Vietnam. However, he was unwilling to use Congress' principal weapon—the power of the purse—to try to bring the war to an end by cutting off funds for it. Similarly, Albert, who has been on the floor much less often than his two predecessors Rayburn and McCormack, is not the type to twist arms to get the votes he needs to override presidential vetoes. Speaker Rayburn used a room opposite the member's dining room in the first floor of the Capitol sometimes called the "Board of Education," as a command post. There, over late afternoon drinks with friends who made up an informal intelligence system, he kept up with the current sentiments of the House. It was in this room also that pressure was applied to wavering party members whose votes were needed. This is in stark contrast to the laissez-faire approach of Albert.

2. *The Feudal Barons: Committee and Subcommittee Chairmen*

Much of the real power in Congress lies not with its formal leaders but with the chairmen of the committees and subcommittees of the House and the Senate. It is important to remember that committee-based influence derives not only from committee chairmanships but also from important subcommittee chairmanships. An unanticipated byproduct of the reduction in the number of standing committees (from forty-eight to nineteen), resulting from the Legislative Reorganization Act of 1946, has been growth in the number and importance of subcommittees. Richard Fenno has pointed out that any analyses of power in the House "which excludes the 123 subcommittees can be but caricatures of the [actual] influence patterns."[14]

In addition to the standing committees there are on occasion select committees appointed to investigate a specific problem. The sudden emergence of Senator Sam J. Ervin, Jr. (D., North Carolina) as a national celebrity came from daily exposure on television as chairman of the Select Senate Committee on Presidential Campaign Activities, which investigated the Watergate affair. Prior to the Watergate hearings Ervin was a well-respected and influential member of the Senate, but unknown to the general public. Much of his influence came from his committee and subcommittee chairmanships. He is chairman of the Government Operations Committee which deals among other things with budget and accounting measures, reorganization of the executive branch, and intergovernmental relationships in the federal system. As third-ranking member on the Judiciary Committee he chairs three subcommittees: Constitutional Rights, Revision and Codification, and Separation of Powers. He also is the fourth-ranking member and a subcommittee chairman on the Armed Services Committee. A lawyer by training, he is one of the nation's leading authorities on the Constitution. It would be hard to think of another senator more strategically placed or better qualified to head up the Watergate investigation. Yet in the spring of 1973, before the Watergate Committee began holding hearings, only 20 per cent of a supposedly politically sophisticated class of Brown University political science students could identify the name "Sam Ervin" on a spot quiz. This is characteristic of much of even the informed public's knowledge of Congress—they know who the speechmakers are but have little idea of who the really effective members are.

In the past the Southerners in the House, under the leadership of the wily Howard W. Smith (D., Virginia), deliberately maneuvered to place at least one of their number on each committee and to keep him there, accruing valuable seniority. For instance, John L. McMillan (D., South Carolina), for many years chairman of the House District of Columbia Committee, remained on that little-sought-after committee for over ten years watching liberal Democrats come and go until he became chairman. From that time (1954) until his defeat in 1972, he had enormous influence over the lives of District residents—many of whom were desperately in need of liberal-initiated social programs. Unfortunately, liberals had fled that committee for the greener pastures of Education and Labor or Banking and Currency, thereby abdicating control of the committee to conservatives.

Better planning on the part of liberals in Congress during the initial assignment process and a greater willingness to remain on the less attractive committees would greatly increase the number of them in seniority positions on a wide range of committees, which are the principal power bases for members trying to develop influence.

Obviously, the chairmen of the most prestigious congressional committees and subcommittees have a strategic advantage. However, even relatively unimportant committees can be turned into power bases by a member of Congress who is willing to exploit their potential to the fullest. A case in point is Wayne L. Hays (D., Ohio) who has emerged as one of the most powerful members of the House. Hays assumed the chairmanship of the lowly House Administration Committee in 1971 and has parlayed his control over House payrolls, personnel, printing, and contracts—none of which attract much outside interest—into an impressive power base. He is also chairman of the Democratic Congressional Campaign Committee which dispenses campaign funds to party candidates. This increases his leverage over a number of congressmen. Always known as a tough, effective—if sometimes acid—debater on the floor, Hays had the insight and political sense to see possibilities in a position many liberal members would have sneered at.

REFORM AND CHANGE

One certainty about Congress is that there will always be people, mostly liberals, calling for its reform. For at least two reasons, however, much of this continuing clamor is unrealistic, particularly from a liberal perspective.

First, a series of major reforms have already taken place. A number of reforms were included in the 1970 Legislative Reorganization Act. The seniority principle has been weakened. Both parties in the House have adopted rules which allow for the party caucuses to vote on committee chairmen and ranking minority members. The Democrats have spread the power positions around more widely by limiting each member (in most cases) to one subcommittee chairmanship. A House select committee, chaired by Richard Bolling (D., Missouri), author of several reform-oriented books on Congress, has been studying the committee system and will report its findings and recommendations to the House in the near future.

In fact, much of the attack on the seniority system by liberal groups at this time is actually self-defeating. The

election of 1946 was marked by a Republican landslide
everywhere but the South and gave the Republicans a
majority in the House for two of the four years they have
been in control since 1932. The practical effect of this one
triumph was to wipe out a Democratic "seniority generation" in the North. It is ironic now that as northern, liberal,
urban congressmen are finally beginning to be the beneficiaries of the seniority system, their adherents in the general
public continue to clamor for changes which will actually
reduce the internal influence of the progressive forces.[15]

The second reason is that it is more important to change
the people in Congress than the rules of Congress. The rules
of Congress are quite flexible and open to many different
interpretations. The most "liberal" rules in the world will
serve little purpose if they govern a body predominantly
composed of conservatives. Changing the personnel of Congress will be undramatic and incremental, but it is the most
effective way of changing the institution. To bring about
needed changes, progressive forces will have to back candidates who not only are good on the issues but also are skillful
legislative politicians adept at alliance politics. The recent
session of the House Democratic Study Group (DSG),
chaired by Representative Burton in the 92nd Congress took a
step in the right direction. Burton, ably assisted by DSG
Staff Director Richard Conlon, expanded the effective DSG
membership significantly and was able to work out compromise positions with old-line "bread-and-butter" liberals on
a number of issues. As Burton put it, "what real good does
it do our side to have one of our guys make his conscience
feel good by delivering a long diatribe on Rhodesia if it
loses us votes for a decent health care program?"

In the Senate, some liberals have indulged in too much
posturing and too little hard work on day-to-day Senate
business. The reason a conservative southern Democrat like
Byrd could become so powerful is that Senate liberals failed
to pay attention to many of the less glamorous aspects of

their job and left a power vacuum which a hard worker like Byrd could convert to his advantage.

The "expressive function" of Congress, to use Woodrow Wilson's phrase, is important. Congress is, in an important sense, the conscience of the nation and should serve as a forum for the articulation of new ideals and the illumination of old realities. But a legislature which concentrates exclusively on debate is in danger of becoming, like the German Reichstag of the 1930s, a "chamber of echoes." The real business of a legislature is legislation, and the real job of an effective legislator is to get things done.

NOTES

1. See William S. White, *The Citadel* (New York: Harper & Row, 1956).
2. Nelson Polsby presents a number of compelling arguments against White's thesis in his *Congress and the Presidency*, 2nd ed. (Englewood Cliffs, N.J.: Prentice-Hall, 1971), pp. 52–61.
3. For a readable discussion of the formal rules of Congress, see Lewis A. Froman, *The Congressional Process* (Boston: Little, Brown, 1967).
4. Donald Matthews, *U. S. Senators and Their World* (Chapel Hill, N.C.: University of North Carolina Press, 1960), discusses the informal "folkways" of the Senate. A more extensive list of informal rules-of-the-game operative in state legislatures, many of which are applicable to Congress, can be found in John Wahlke, et al., *The Legislative System* (New York: Wiley, 1962).
5. For evidence on the decline of apprenticeship, see Herbert Asher, "The Learning of Legislative Norms,"

American Political Science Review, June 1973, pp. 323–38.

6. See Richard F. Fenno, *The Power of the Purse: Appropriation Politics in Congress* (Boston: Little, Brown, 1966).

7. Roger Davidson, *The Role of the Congressman* (New York: Pegasus, 1969), p. 23.

8. Richard Neustadt, *Presidential Power: The Politics of Leadership* (New York: Wiley, 1960), p. 22.

9. Ralph K. Huitt, "The Outsider in the Senate: An Alternative Role," *American Political Science Review,* 55 (September 1961), p. 575.

10. Nicholas Masters, "Committee Assignments in the House of Representatives," *American Political Science Review,* 55 (June 1961), pp. 351–55.

11. Nelson Polsby, "Two Strategies of Influence: Choosing a Majority Leader, 1962," in Robert Peabody and Nelson Polsby, *New Perspectives on the House of Representatives,* 2nd ed. (Chicago: Rand McNally 1969), p. 342.

12. See Robert L. Peabody, "Party Leadership Change in the U. S. House of Representatives," *American Political Science Review,* 61 (September 1967), pp. 675–93.

13. Randall Ripley, "The Party Whip Organizations in the U. S. House of Representatives," *American Political Science Review,* 57 (September 1964), pp. 561–76.

14. Richard F. Fenno, "The Internal Distribution of Influence: The House," in David B. Truman, *The Congress and America's Future* (Englewood Cliffs, N.J. Prentice-Hall, 1965), p. 55.

15. See Raymond E. Wolfinger and Joan Heifetz, "Safe Seats, Seniority, and Power in Congress," *American Political Science Review,* 59 (June 1965), pp. 337–49.

CHAPTER 3

WHAT CAN VOLUNTEER ACTIVITY MEAN?
A CASE STUDY OF 1970

Whether or not citizen-activists can have a significant impact on the American political system depends in large part upon the willingness of people with the available time and inclination to become involved. In 1970, students, more than any other group, played this role. Their successes and failures illustrate well both the potentials and pitfalls of working within the system.

THE REACTION TO CAMBODIA AND KENT STATE:
A Movement is Born

On the evening of April 30, 1970, President Richard M. Nixon went before a nationwide television audience to announce that he had ordered American troops to attack Communist sanctuaries in the frontier area of Cambodia in order to expedite the withdrawal of American troops from Vietnam.

On American college campuses feelings about the Vietnam war were already high. Many students and faculty members anticipated that the broadcast, which had been announced several days earlier, would be related to a new

American escalation of the war. Their worst fears were confirmed, and in the days immediately following the President's speech student strikes and protests were held at a
number of universities and colleges across the country.

When the Cambodia invasion was followed by the murders
of students at Kent State University and Jackson State
College the protests spread. A number of institutions were
forced to cancel or curtail the remainder of the spring
semester.[1]

Student reaction took a variety of forms. Some students
called for campus demonstrations and another "march on
Washington," Others organized resistance to the draft. A
small number engaged in "trashings" and other acts of vio-
lence. Other students organized group discussions and teach-
ins in order "to raise their consciousness"—but did little to
end the war.

There was another notable feature of the campus reaction
that spring besides its size and intensity. For the first time
large numbers of students seemed eager to engage in "in-
the-system" political activities in an attempt to bring the
war to a halt. Newspapers and media accounts were filled
with stories of previously non-involved students who "were
willing to give the system one last chance" by working in
the 1970 Congressional elections.

Students and faculty descended on Washington to lobby
congressmen and senators on war-related issues. Several
groups were set up to raise campaign funds for antiwar House
and Senate candidates.[2]

The Movement for a New Congress (MNC), for example
originated in Princeton University and soon spread to more
than 450 campuses all over the country. Its purpose was to
supply antiwar candidates for Congress with large number
of student volunteer campaign workers.[3]

The MNC aroused quite a bit of interest in the press and
media. Much of this was the result of an early MNC decision

to computerize its volunteer name lists. The computer lent a certain professional, scientific (if misleading) mystique to the whole operation and the interest of the media, who saw a story, and politicians, who saw some readily accessible, free manpower, was thereby intensified.

There were several other reasons for the large amount of publicity MNC received in its early stages. One was the accidental factor of timing—Princeton was the first major college or university to go on strike. The news stories the morning following President Nixon's announcement carried reports of the strike decision, and as more and more schools followed suit, Princeton gained a certain psychological primacy and legitimacy among the many schools and groups which began organizing antiwar activities. Further, the proximity of Princeton to the country's principal media center, New York, undoubtedly increased the chances that the Princeton activities, if deemed "newsworthy," would get ample exposure.

A Democratic primary in a nearby congressional district (15th Dist., New Jersey), pitting a young "dove" challenger, Lew Kaden, against a four-term incumbent "hawk," Edward Patten, provided the first test for the MNC. Kaden was soundly trounced. This was not altogether unexpected by the MNC leadership who regarded the Kaden campaign as a useful means for retaining momentum and working out MNC operational kinks. In fact the Kaden race violated one of the basic guidelines of the MNC—that the organization would go "where the ducks are" and get involved only in "marginal" races. This guideline was adopted because it was believed, on the basis of some scattered and not completely comparable studies, that extensive door-to-door canvassing (the principal campaign skill MNC could provide) could add from 3 to 10 per cent to a candidate's share of the vote.[4] Therefore MNC should only get involved in races in which they could provide their candi-

dates with most of the extra margin they needed to win
In the Kaden-Patten battle, the incumbent had too great a
margin at the start for canvassing to overcome.

Despite some initial setbacks, MNC-backed candidates
scored a number of impressive Democratic primary triumphs
several of them defeating very senior incumbents. For ex
ample, in Maryland Paul S. Sarbanes defeated George H
Fallon who had twenty-eight years seniority in the House
and Parren J. Mitchell defeated Samuel N. Friedel who
had eighteen years; in Colorado Byron G. Rogers, a twenty
year veteran, lost in a primary to Craig Barnes; in Massa
chusetts an antiwar Jesuit priest, Robert F. Drinan, unseated
thirteen-term Congressman Philip J. Philbin.

WHAT CAN VOLUNTEERS DO?

There have been a number of studies of the noisier an
sometimes violent "young radicals" but few investigation
of the motivations and activities of radical youth workin
"in the system." Although the work of the latter has no
been as dramatic as that of their extremist counterparts, man
have played critical roles in our recent national elections be
ginning, at least, with the 1968 presidential primary cam
paigns of Eugene McCarthy and Robert Kennedy.

It was estimated by *Congressional Quarterly* that in 197(
75,000 students had worked for MNC-associated candidate
in both the primaries and the general elections.[5] This figure
of course, does not represent the entire scope of student i
volvement in those elections. Conservative "hawks" like Gov
ernor Ronald Reagan in California and James L. Buckley
who was running for the Senate in New York, also had larg
contingents of youthful volunteers. Postelection surveys b
the Gallup Organization of nationwide samples placed th
participation rates between 10 and 15 per cent of the tota
college population. While not quite the hordes envisioned i

the euphoric, if unrealistic, press forecasts of the spring, this nevertheless represented between 700,000 and one million people—probably the largest outpouring of nonparty organization volunteers in our electoral history.

The decline of the big-city machines and party organizations has depleted the principal source of manpower for grass-roots campaign activities.[6] An interesting paradox of the New Politics is that while its practitioners reject the style and values of the Old Politics, they have combined many of the old political *techniques* (e.g., extensive door-to-door canvassing) with those of a newer age (e.g., computerized mailings and sophisticated media use).

Where will the leg-power for grass-roots activities, so critical to the New Politics, come from? At present there are three major pools of potential volunteers—students, housewives (mainly suburban, upper-middle class), and some labor unions.[7] The most likely of the three in terms of time availability, are the students. Moreover, the good internal communication systems at most colleges makes organizing simpler. Students living on campus can be reached relatively easily, and as they are geographically close to each other, they can be more effectively mobilized than other groups in the society.

This pool of student volunteers is a potentially important resource for almost any campaign, especially so when it can be used to compensate for other, less available resources like money. In national campaigns this can be especially critical in the early stages for a candidate with relatively little money and a low name-recognition factor.

In early 1972 Senator George McGovern's student volunteers, fewer in number but much more efficiently organized than the "Clean for Gene" kids of 1968, kept his presidential primary campaign afloat in New Hampshire. At that point, he had received few campaign donations and was not well known to the general public. Without this volunteer aid he would undoubtedly have had to drop out of the race very early on.

In trying to assess just what student volunteers can contribute to a campaign it is misleading simply to examine the won-lost rates of candidates who used student volunteers or who received the endorsement of campus-oriented organizations. Rather, volunteers should be assessed as one of a number of short-term variables that affect voters' decisions. The cumulative effect of these forces results in greater or lesser deviations from the long-run standing party divisions of the American electorate.[8]

Studies of the impact of personal contact on voters indicate that good party workers can increase voter turnout and can add up to 5 per cent to their candidate's vote over what could be expected on the basis of the "normal vote." Even greater gains (about 10 per cent) have been found in districts where one party's workers were significantly more effective than the other party's.

Table III presents data showing the impact MNC student volunteers had on the turnout and preference rates of voters in six 1970 congressional races which had high degrees of student involvement.[9]

Table III

Impact of Contact by MNC Volunteers
on Voter Turnout and Preference

	CONTACTED	NOT CONTACTED
Voted	87.1	81.3
Did not vote	12.9	18.7
Voted for MNC-backed candidate	77.8	64.4
Voted for his opponent	22.2	32.6

By "turnout" effect we mean the differences in the turnout rates between individuals who were personally contacted by MNC volunteers and a control group of voters living in the same precincts who were not contacted. "Preference" effect indicates the difference between the two groups in their support of the MNC candidate.[10]

The turnout rate was almost 6 per cent higher for the individuals who were personally contacted than for those who were not contacted. Door-to-door canvassing increased the peace candidate's share of the vote even more—10.4 per cent.

The impact of the MNC door-to-door canvassing on voter turnout and preference varied, however, among different categories of voters. Table IV shows the effect of contact by a MNC worker on five categories of voters. The basic MNC hypothesis was that personal contact would have the greatest effect among those voters who, in the absence of such contact, would normally possess the least information about the candidates and be the least likely to vote.

With one exception, the canvassing showed the greatest impact on turnout among those who had the weakest party indentification. This would be expected, as the studies have shown that the stronger a voter's sense of identification with a party, the greater the probability that he will vote.

The exception was among strong Republicans, who showed the greatest turnout effect. The rates at which Republicans supported the MNC-backed candidates in the sample were also substantially increased by personal contact by a door-to-door worker.

Here then, is one of the major ways in which volunteer activities can have a substantial impact on elections. Other voting studies have shown that the acquisition of even some information about the opposite party's candidate can result in substantial deviations from party voting. In their study of the 1958 congressional elections, for example, Miller and Stokes showed that party identifiers who had no information about either candidate opted for the candidate of their own party 92 per cent of the time, while virtually all (98 per cent) of those who only knew something about the candidate of their own party voted for him. However, four out of ten of those voters who only knew something about the opposing party's candidate defected and voted contrary to their party allegiance.[11]

Table IV

The Impact of MNC Volunteer Contact on Turnout and
Preference Rates of Selected Groups of Voters

		Turnout Increase	Preference Increase
A.	*Party Identification*		
	DEMOCRAT	2.0%	4.3%
	WEAK DEMOCRAT	6.6	14.3
	INDEPENDENT	8.6	3.9
	WEAK REPUBLICAN	6.0	17.2
	REPUBLICAN	13.6	15.3
B.	*Sex*		
	MALE	11.1	9.4
	FEMALE	13.7	11.4
C.	*Age*		
	21–30 YEARS	6.4	17.2
	31–40 YEARS	4.7	11.5
	41–50 YEARS	10.5	7.5
	51–60 YEARS	1.6	11.8
	61 AND OVER	1.6	4.6
D.	*Position on War*		
	DOVE	9.1	15.3
	QUALIFIED	0.8	4.8
	HAWK	4.2	−4.4

	Turnout Increase	Preference Increase
E. *Opinion of Student Electoral Participation*		
GOOD IDEA	3.4	8.9
NOT SURE	0.1	12.7
BAD IDEA	18.8	4.3

Personal contact increased both women's turnout and preference rates slightly more than men's. This would be expected from what we know from previous studies about women's political participation. In general, women turn out to vote less than men and have less information about the candidates. There are a number of reasons for the differences in the political participation of the two sexes. Our society has traditionally defined women's roles as secondary and submissive. Older women lagged behind their male peers in education while many younger women are saddled with the responsibilities of raising small children and running a home.[12]

Age has also been found to have a close association with citizens' political participation. The greatest turnout effect occurred among the middle-age group (forty-one to fifty years) with the second largest among the youngest voters. The increase in the turnout of the two oldest groups was barely perceptible.

The MNC contacts added a substantial increment (17.2 per cent) to their candidate's share of the youngest voters. One would expect the youngest voters, many of whom were peers of the MNC volunteers in age and life style, to respond most to contact by the volunteers. In addition, youngest voters are the most fluid and volatile age group in terms of party preferences and therefore their choice of candidates would be more likely to be influenced by short-term forces like personal contact. The other age groups all showed smaller but positive preference effects.

Table IV also breaks the voter sample down in terms of their position on the Vietnam war. The strongest turnout effect occurred among doves. Contact with canvassers with similar views on the war undoubtedly reinforced and strengthened the intentions of many doves to vote. Moreover, many of the persons identified as doves in the MNC canvasses received additional encouragement to vote as part of "get out the vote" operations on Election Day.

Doves also showed the greatest preference effect. This, again, is partly a function of "pulling" operations on Election Day, designed to get as many voters to the polls as possible who had been identified as sympathetic to the candidate. Personal contact also had a strong effect on doves because large proportions of the social groups least likely to vote—especially women, blacks, and lower-status individuals—had been reported as holding dovish views at the time of the 1970 elections.[13] In off-year (non-presidential) elections, which are marked by low citizen interest, such people would be even less likely to participate. But once mobilized by personal contact by a campaign worker for a dove candidate, they represented a substantial, unexpected bonus for him.

People with hawkish views on the war were the only group that showed a negative preference effect. Hawks who had been contacted by MNC volunteers voted for the dove candidate 4.4 per cent *less* than hawks who were not contacted. If we compare the turnout and preference effects of hawks, we see that they are of about equal magnitude but opposite in sign.

What may have occurred here is a "stirring up the hornet's nest" situation, in which a greater than usual proportion of hawkish voters—many of whom already opposed the dove candidate—turned out to vote after becoming aware, through contact with a MNC canvasser, that a vigorous campaign was being waged by the dove candidate.

This was not a case of "youth lash" in which dove candidates were damaged by using students as campaign workers.

Talk of such a youth lash in the 1970 congressional elections was quite common among politicians and the news media at the time. In addition, many of the speeches of some Administration figures, notably Vice President Agnew and Attorney General Mitchell, contained a great deal of antiyouth sentiment. In June 1970 campus unrest ranked first in the Gallup Poll as the major problem facing the country—ahead of war in Vietnam, race relations, inflation, and unemployment. The conjunction of the concern about campus unrest and the prospect that large numbers of students would, after the Cambodian invasion, work for peace candidates in the congressional elections, raised the specter of a backlash against young political workers.

For a youth lash to occur several conditions must be met. A voter must (1) either perceive one candidate as taking "proyouth" issue positions or, regardless of the candidate's issue positions, perceive that candidate's campaign workers who contact him as students and then (2) cast his vote *for* the candidate associated with antistudent positions or antiyouth positions or *against* the candidate associated with prostudent positions; (3) he must also have been undecided as to whom to vote for or to have favored the youth-supported candidates prior to (1) and (2).

Part of this postelection study of the 1970 congressional elections dealt with the problem of youth lash. The findings have some very practical import for future campaigns relying on a large volunteer effort because many of these volunteers will be young people.

It was found that only about one third of those who had been contacted by a student worker could positively identify the person contacting them as a student. The other two thirds of those contacted by student workers did not identify the person contacting them as a student or young person—most remembered the canvassers simply as party workers or could not remember who it was that contacted them.

Not shown in Table IV is the finding that an overwhelming proportion of the voters felt it was a good idea for students to be involved in electoral politics. Negative attitudes toward campus dissent, drugs, and student life style were not translated into negative feelings about students working for congressional candidates. Of those who originally favored the dove candidate or were undecided, who recognized the canvasser as a student, who disapproved of student involvement, and who comprised the only group among whom a backlash against students could possibly occur, only a tiny fraction (less than 1 per cent) felt that the student contact had had a negative effect on their vote.

The final category of Table IV correlates increases in voter turnout and preference with voters' opinions about young people working in electoral politics. The largest increase in turnout was registered among voters who disapproved of students working in political campaigns. But this did not lead those who disapproved of student involvement to vote against the peace candidates. In fact, among the group who disapproved of student involvement the dove candidate's share of the vote was 4.3 per cent higher for those who were contacted by MNC volunteers than for those who were not contacted. Contacted voters who approved of or were not sure about student participation showed even greater increases in their vote for the peace candidate.

THE LESSONS OF 1970:
A Summing Up

The involvement of thousands of college students in the 1970 congressional elections had a number of important results. A number of progressive new faces were added in the House. Some like Representative James Abourezk (D., South Dakota), who attributed his 1970 victory to the work of 800 Carleton students who were bused over a thousand miles to work for him, have gone on to the Senate. Others like Les Aspin (D., Wisconsin), who has established himself as an

articulate, well-briefed critic of Pentagon spending procedures, have carved out important places for themselves in the
House as experts on specific policy areas. Some others who
lost in 1970, like Gerry E. Studds of Massachusetts, continued to build on their 1970 base and triumphed in 1972.

The volunteer electoral activities of 1970 had another, less
obvious, effect besides increasing voter turnout and the number of votes for dove candidates. A number of congressmen
who had consistently been hawks changed their position after
stiff challenges in primaries by candidates with large volunteer forces. For example, John J. Rooney (D., New York),
Edward Patten (D., New Jersey), and James A. Byrne
(D., Pennsylvania)—three prototypical big-city, "bread-and
butter"-liberals—all had been ardent supporters of the Vietnam war. But even though they successfully fended off their
primary challengers, they subsequently began to vote like
doves.

Before the primaries, professors and students who went to
Washington and presented the most logical, cogent arguments about why the United States should withdraw from
Vietnam had had little effect on such congressmen, who lis-
tened politely to the arguments in their offices and continued
to support the war. But the prospect of alienating a major
faction in their district who were willing to slug it out with
them in a primary and who possibly would work against
them in the general election was another matter.

An elected politician knows that he has to listen to people
who are willing and able to get involved in the hard work of
electoral politics to further their aims or he won't stay in
office much longer. For this reason, and not because of some
late-blooming misgivings about the war, men like Rooney,
Patten, and Byrne became doves.

The 1970 elections also showed, however, that to be effective, volunteer activists have to be well organized and able to
compromise. Moreover, they have to be willing to forsake
the lure of working in hopeless races for attractive candidates

and instead put their energies to work for candidates who have a good possibility of winning. The 1970 elections proved that volunteer activists could play important roles in the American elections. They will continue to be an important factor in our elections—as long as they strive to be effective rather than expressive, flexible rather than rigid.

NOTES

1. For a discussion of the reaction on American college campuses in the spring of 1970, see Richard E. Peterson and John A. Bilorusky, *May, 1970: The Campus Aftermath of Cambodia and Kent State* (New York: Carnegie Foundation, 1971); Sidney Hyman, *Youth in Politics; Expectations and Realities* (New York: Basic Books, 1972).

2. The Academic and Professional Alliance and the Continuing Presence in Washington stressed lobbying while the National Petition Committee and Universities' National Anti-War Fund did fund-raising.

3. The activities of the five major peace groups involved in electoral action were co-ordinated by the National Coalition for a Responsible Congress chaired by Professor James David Barber, now of Duke University.

4. For a summary of some of this literature, see William J. Crotty, "Party Effort and Its Impact on the Vote," *American Political Science Review*, 65 (June 1971), pp. 439–50.

5. *Congressional Quarterly Weekly Report*, October 29, 1970, pp. 2691–92.

6. See, for instance, Raymond Wolfinger, "Why Political Machines Have Not Withered Away and Other Revisionist Thoughts," *Journal of Politics*, May 1972, pp. 365–98; Fred I. Greenstein, *The American Party System and the American People*, 2nd ed. (Englewood Cliffs, N.Y.: Prentice-Hall, 1970), Ch. 4.

7. Very few labor unions still provide significant manpower for electoral activities on behalf of candidates they support. The most active in 1970 were the United Auto Workers and, in some areas, the Steelworkers.

8. For a discussion of some of these aspects of the Survey Research Center's model of voting, see Donald E. Stokes, "Some Dynamic Elements of Contests for the Presidency," *American Political Science Review*, 60 (March 1966), pp. 19–28; Philip E. Converse, "The Concept of the Normal Vote," in Angus Campbell, et al., *Elections and the Political Order* (New York: Wiley, 1966), Ch. 2.

9. The MNC-backed candidates were two incumbent Democrats: Frank Thompson, Jr. (4th Dist., New Jersey) and Henry Helstoski (9th Dist., New Jersey); and four non-incumbent Democrats: Paul Sarbanes (3rd Dist., Maryland), Les Aspin (1st Dist., Wisconsin), John Cihon (6th Dist., Michigan) and former Congressman John Dow (27th Dist., New York). All but Cihon were victorious; he lost to incumbent Republican Charles E. Chamberlain.

10. The contacted group and the control group did not differ significantly in terms of their party identification rates, age, sex, or issue positions. Moreover, as both groups resided in the same precincts, they were not subject to differential environmental effects.

11. Donald E. Stokes and Warren E. Miller, "Party Government and the Saliency of Congress," in Campbell, et al., op. cit., pp. 204–5.

12. See Campbell, et al., *The American Voter* (New York: Wiley, 1960).

13. Sidney Verba and Richard A. Brody, "Participation, Policy, Preferences, and the War in Vietnam," *Public Opinion Quarterly*, 34 (Fall 1970), pp. 325–32.

CHAPTER 4

GETTING STARTED IN ELECTORAL POLITICS

Once you have decided that you want to go into politics, how do you get started? The answer, surprisingly, is not easy. There are, to begin with, enormous differences between regions and, within them, between campaigns. Many campaign organizations are so accustomed to citizen apathy and so poorly managed that they simply do not know what to do with people who come in to volunteer their help.

Most volunteers enter the campaign picture late in the game. The candidates, as a rule, have already filed or been nominated, the basic strategies have been defined and major job responsibilities determined. By the time you walk into headquarters (if there is one), the problems of coping with their day-to-day responsibilities make many full-time campaign workers at best impatient, at worst downright hostile to "strangers." Some campaign managers, moreover, simply do not believe that volunteer campaign workers are very useful. Some argue, for example, that in this media age the campaign amateur has been displaced in favor of the professional public relations team. Others prefer to rely upon existing party organizations and paid workers. Their argument, which all too often turns out to be correct, is that volunteer activists tend to be unreliable to the point of being more trouble than help. Stories abound—

—of a campaign manager who spent two valuable hours training and briefing four volunteer canvassers only to have them quit in discouragement after having three doors slammed in their faces;

—of a financially pressed candidate who accepted the offer of a local sports club to put out a mailing. Having turned over the key to his headquarters to the club members, he returned the next morning to find that they had papered one wall of the offices with the 2,500 last-remaining bumper stickers on hand in headquarters. Figuring at 8 cents per bumper sticker, plus the cost of forfeiting his damage deposit to the landlord, the candidate calculated that he could have saved $100 by having the mailing prepared by Office Temporaries;

—of an enthusiastic but clumsy volunteer who managed in two hours to bend, fold, spindle, and mutilate 22,000 valuable computer cards and who quit in tears soon after;

—of two enthusiastic door-to-door workers who combined their pitch for the candidate in a blue-collar Catholic neighborhood with an argument favoring a federal law to legalize abortion.

So we revert to Rule 1: *Don't be discouraged*. Don't be discouraged if your help is not welcomed with flowers, flags, huzzahs, and open arms. Don't be discouraged if the candidate or his aides treat you like some kind of a nut.

In a general election (as opposed to a primary) there are more ways than one to volunteer your services. If the individual candidate is not particularly receptive, you may be able to work through the party organization. Local precinct captains, ward leaders, district committeemen and committeewomen, or whatever they are called in your state are usually quite anxious for help. You can get their names from the county or municipal clerk. And the party leader for your county or city may have districts which he feels are inadequately covered and welcome help. This usually means, of course, that although you can give special attention to your favorite candidate, you must work the whole party ticket.

Primary campaigns are more difficult. They are, to begin with, shorter and less well organized. The regular party organizations, moreover, are likely either to take a hands-off attitude (in many states they are prohibited by law from working in primaries) or to be on the "wrong" side. The important thing here—as well, really, as in the general election —is to present yourself as seriously interested in working. Don't just waltz in saying, "Here I am, you lucky devils." Bring, if you can, a schedule of times during which you are available to work, a list of specific skills and experiences, and an idea of the kinds of things you would (a) like, (b) be willing, and (c) grudgingly agree to do.

The remainder of this chapter is directed primarily toward those who are in on the ground floor of a campaign. It is a brief guide to the first steps of launching a new candidate. Those readers who plan to work for incumbents or who come late into a campaign may wish to skip to Chapter 5, unless they want to understand the steps which have preceded them and shaped the context within which they will work.

WHY WORK WITHIN THE EXISTING PARTIES?

The temptation to say the hell with the existing party structures and strike out on an independent course is always strong. It should be resisted not out of historical reverence for the two-party system so much as out of hard-nosed realism. Early in his 1973 unsuccessful campaign to be mayor of New York, Assemblyman Albert Blumenthal ruefully charged that if liberals were asked to form a firing squad, the first order would be "Form a circle!"

The best reason for working within the existing two-party

system is often founded in simple mathematics. Suppose that in the mythical state of Wahoo 25 per cent of the voters are Far Lefties, 25 per cent Middle Lefties, 10 per cent Independents and Fuzzyheads, 20 per cent Middle Righties, and 20 per cent Far Righties. Anytime both groups of Lefties agree on a candidate, they need only one independent vote to be sure of winning. Only if all four right and left parties disagree with one another does any one of them have a chance of winning on its own. That chance is based on winning a plurality of the Independent and Fuzzyhead votes—a thin reed to lean upon, particularly in the more extreme factions. The only road to power in Wahoo for either the Far Left or the Far Right is to win control of an existing party, and, hopefully, keep it intact.

What independent or third-party candidacies can do at best is to punish an inflexible organization. Third party candidates almost never win. The bizarre election laws of New York State that helped James L. Buckley of New York win a Senate seat on the Conservative line and the personal meaning of the Byrd name in Byrdland (sometimes known as Virginia) that helped elect Harry F. Byrd, Jr., are the exceptions that prove the rule. Prior to the Byrd and Buckley victories in 1970, the last person to win a seat in either house of Congress without major party endorsement was Representative H. Frazier Reams of Ohio, who won as an Independent in 1953. (Former Senator Wayne Morse of Oregon *served* briefly as an Independent in the Senate, but switched to the Democratic party in time for the 1956 election.) What a third-party candidate or independent can from time to time do is to take away enough votes from a major party candidate to insure the election of his opponent. As opposed to the "lesser-evilism" of working for a candidate with whom one only partially agrees, working for a third-party candidate or independent in this case might be called "greater-evilism," or, in Blumenthal's phrase, "forming a circle."

FINDING CANDIDATES

Suppose that an incumbent retires, that you are in the out party, or that you feel that the time has come to launch a primary challenge. What next? The first problem, obviously, is to find a candidate. "Movements" per se can neither win elections, find places on the ballot, or serve in office. You must have a warm body, preferably a live one. Obviously, it is important that your candidate meet the legal requirements of residence, age, citizenship, and voter registration. Nothing can be more embarrassing—as New Jersey's 13th District Democrats discovered in 1972—than to have your candidate ruled off the ballot on a technicality. (In the New Jersey case, the candidate failed to meet the Constitutional requirement that he be "seven years a citizen of the United States.")

Beyond legal criteria, surveys have shown that the electorate tends to have rather definite notions of personal characteristics that they find desirable in a candidate. Although the questions asked in different surveys are not always comparable, David Leuthold has summarized these preferred qualities as follows:

Most important characteristic
    Experience

Next most important characteristics
    Honesty, integrity
    Education, intelligence

Frequently mentioned characteristics
    Independence, decisiveness
    Leadership, administrative ability
    Aggressiveness, strength
    Youth, energy, good health
    Nice personality
    Family man, good family life (not divorced)[1]

There are four other characteristics, not explicitly mentioned in these surveys, which deserve consideration. It helps, to begin with, if the candidate has local roots. Better than nine out of ten members of the House of Representatives were born in the states they represent and more than half still reside in the towns in which they were born. Whatever sterling characteristics your candidate may possess count for naught if nobody knows him or her.

Related to the question of origins is the problem of prominence. A locally known family name—as John (no relation) Kennedy proved when he was elected state treasurer in Massachusetts—helps. Those who have previously run for office, and better yet won, usually have recognizable names. So do people in certain occupations, such as real estate agents whose signs cover the district or the leaders of important interest groups.

The remaining two characteristics have less to do with public images than with the campaign itself, but they are probably the most important of all. First, the candidate has to be able to get along well with other people, to be able to respect and trust their judgment. This is particularly important in a volunteer campaign where the continued activity of the staff depends less on tangible rewards than on faith, admiration, respect, and even love.

> The candidate must have confidence in the staff's ability to run the campaign, as he cannot run it himself. Likewise, the staff must have confidence in the candidate and his ability to see the issues and the problems of the campaign.[2]

In the long run the candidate's ability to get along with his staff may be even more important than the image he projects in public appearances. Dick Simpson has this advice for campaign workers:

> Don't be overly sensitive about shortcomings of your candidate's personality, especially since he or she will usually

meet (for more than a handshake at the bus stop) only
one, or two thousand voters. A candidate is most important for recruiting workers and raising money. It is the
workers who have the greater contact with individual
voters. If your candidate is able to capture the support
of potential workers, he will be able to learn during the
campaign itself the necessary techniques to appeal to
voters.[3]

The most important qualification of all is that the candidate have time. Campaigning is a full-time job. It would be
nice, for example, if there were more blue-collar workers
running for Congress, but a candidate cannot serve two
masters. He cannot be out early in the morning meeting factory workers if he has to punch a clock himself. He cannot
put out campaign fires if he is not accessible by phone at
every hour. He cannot plan strategies and work with his staff
if he has to get to bed early every night. He cannot speak at
an out-of-town Rotary Club lunch if he works in the city. He
cannot get a good press if he cannot meet reporters and editors during their working hours.

Woodrow Wilson once said that we were moving toward
a system of government which would be ruled by wealthy,
intelligent athletes—a small class indeed. Worse yet, many
of those who fit Wilson's bill wouldn't even consider risking
the possible loss of wealth or status to run for office. It
should not be too surprising to find that many incumbents
in Congress will run in 1974, as they have in the past, without significant opposition.

One of the reasons for candidate reluctance can, however,
be overcome: the costs of a campaign. It takes a lot of money
—if only for baby-sitters, transportation, and luncheons—
even to lose. Some of these costs can be reduced by good
organization. Though many, if not most, candidates run for
a variety of reasons besides the desire to hold office—for ego
gratification, to advertise themselves, say, as lawyers, to get
out of the house—serious ones run because they want to

win, and winning requires at least two things: good organization and money. The group that can promise these resources may be able to persuade an otherwise reluctant individual to risk plunging into expensive political waters. If you can get fifty people each to pledge both to work fifty hours and raise $500, you may be able to persuade your man or your woman that he or she can afford a good hard campaign.

BUILDING AN ORGANIZATION

Politics is a process of building coalitions. It involves tamping down differences and stressing commonalities. Candidates provide the crucial focal points in this process, but there is a sense in which the process both precedes and follows all campaigns. Joe Hill's plea, "Don't mourn for me, organize!" should be emblazoned in the heart of every serious volunteer activist.

Unfortunately, it doesn't usually work that way. Each campaign, it seems, starts from scratch. The conservative activists who dominated Republican nominating conventions and primaries in 1964 were seldom to be found in 1966. Eugene McCarthy's 1968 army of volunteers which helped him win several primaries over President Johnson had disappeared by campaign time for a new Congress in 1970.

Good politics is also a matter of good lists. A key to successful political organizing is the ability, over a long period of time, to be able to identify as precisely as possible all potential pockets of support. This, historically, was the function of the ward or precinct worker; each district committeeman or woman was supposed to be able to predict within a few votes the outcome of every primary and general election simply because they knew how everybody in the area voted. This situation has changed. The decline of party machines has weakened incentives for volunteer workers, the increased mobility of the populace has made knowledge of neighborhoods more difficult, the expanded incidence of ticket-split-

ting has made prediction virtually impossible. Instead of the
neighborhood, the functional group has become the major
source of voting lists.

Four kinds of lists are of particular importance in building
a political organization or running a campaign. First and
most basic is the list of registered voters. Every state, in some
form or another, at some time or another, has such lists. The
most useful are those which provide information on party
preferences—either because registration is by party or because voting in a party's primary automatically produces a
listing under that label. This kind of list has two major shortcomings. (1) In general elections, it is not a reliable guide to
actual voting behavior. Particularly in the South or in areas
of heavy southern in-migration like Southern California or
New Mexico, for example, the habit of registering as a Democrat often hides a marked tendency to vote Republican.
(2) It is not a reliable guide to the future—last year's guide
to party preference may not reflect this year's thinking. Those
registered as independents or who list no party preference
at all are susceptible to the appeals of any strong new
politics candidate. In states like Oregon and Wisconsin, cross-
over voting is permitted in primaries, which compounds the
problem in those states.

The second important kind of list is that compiled in a
previous campaign. For progressive candidates running in
1974, the canvassing sheets of the McGovern presidential
campaign will be invaluable if they can be found. Incumbents have a tremendous advantage in this regard, the nui-
sance of transferring lists from one-year's campaign to the
next, does not occur for them.

A third important kind of list is of special groups. These
are often difficult to acquire, but they can be of enormous
value for fund raising, mail campaigns, and special events.
Some lists are fairly easy to compile—for doctors, for example, try the Yellow Pages. Lists of union members, teach-
ers, college students and faculty, peace group members,

farmers, veterans, senior citizens, or Elks may be more difficult to obtain. If available, however, they provide means of
contact that can be of vital importance.

Mailings have until recently been a waste of money: buried
among the bills, and junk mail, form letters from candidates
quickly found their way into the circular file. There is,
however, a good chance that a union member will read a
letter from the leader of his local, that a lawyer will read
what a fellow lawyer has to say, and that a veteran will
have some interest in what your candidate has to say about
veteran's affairs. Because of its ability to sort quickly and
"personalize" each letter, the growing sophistication of computer technology has now made direct mail a rival to television in its impact on modern campaigns.[4] But although
machines can sort and classify information into whatever
groupings you want, they cannot compile the lists.[5]

A fourth and often overlooked list is that compiled during
the campaign itself. In most states, petitions signed with
names and addresses must be filed and verified in order to
place a candidate's name on the ballot. The required number of signatures is usually small; but the process of gathering them is good for training door-to-door volunteers and
significantly to exceed the required number helps build momentum for the campaign ahead. (It is prudent if not necessary to exceed the legal requirement by at least 50 per cent
anyway since many signatures are likely to be ruled invalid).
Petition signatures are relatively easy to get—some people
will sign damn near anything and most can be persuaded
that your candidate has the right to run. John Gilligan of
Ohio started his career in politics by gathering 40,000 signatures on petitions supporting his candidacy for the House
of Representatives. This list, fed into the computer, can become the core of a mailing list and an important starting
point for later canvassing activities, fund-raising appeals, and
special events. Some candidates send each petition signer a
questionnaire seeking attitudes on important issues. Although

such polls are not scientifically reliable, they can be used to identify voters according to their policy preferences. Many incumbents use the device of polling their constituents as a means of augmenting their mailing lists.

It is generally a good rule to use every available device to build and refine your lists and to follow up every individual contact with a personal letter. (At a very minimum, every voter who signs a petition, contributes money, drops by the headquarters, or attends a reception should get a letter of thanks from their candidate.) Used with door-to-door canvassing, your lists obviously enable you to maximize the impact of your candidate's campaign and election day activities.

Having located and identified potential supporters, the next important step in building an organization is to involve as many people as possible in the campaign. Participation, even to the minimal extent of contributing a dollar, wearing a button, or attending a meeting, gives people a sense of involvement that is likely to firm up loyalties. Any device that increases involvement of a voter you should regard as an opportunity to increase support for your candidate. To turn down an offer to help, conversely, may be to turn off a potential voter. One campaign consultant goes so far as to suggest that headquarters be supplied with a useless stack of envelopes to be addressed by people walking in and volunteering to help at times when there is nothing really for them to do. Even if the envelopes are later thrown away, the activist base of the campaign has been extended.

Whether or not busy work must be provided, the essence of building an effective organization is involving large numbers of people in meaningful activities. Campaigns, like other organizations, develop problems of status, power, and role. Keeping the organization together will take many hours of valuable time (much of it the candidate's) and involve many bruised egos. No matter how much solidarity there is at the outset, no matter how well everyone gets along, no matter how great their common commitment to the cause, jealousy, frustration, and even rage are as much a part of politics as bumper stickers. A major source of tension can be conflicting roles; these must be carefully defined. To the outside world, the campaign must speak with a single voice: there can only be one press secretary, the person whom the press can rely upon and find, the person who can officially articulate "the party line." Similarly, if cash outflow is to match income in some reasonable way, there must be a single person in charge of the campaign checkbook. And, most importantly, there must be a place where the "buck finally stops"—a single campaign manager whose job it is to enforce all major policy decisions, determine roles and jobs, set schedules, and basically run the campaign.

The time of the candidate is simply too valuable for him or her to be too intimately involved in day-to-day operational decisions. An unfortunate by-product of this rule is a tendency for campaigns to take on a peculiarly schizophrenic character in the sense that the candidate becomes almost a dehumanized commodity to be marketed and sold. Speech writers wince as the candidate stumbles over their words. Press agents blanch as he talks off the cuff to an untrustworthy reporter. Municipal or ward leaders vie for the candidate's body: just one more day in Mudville and we can lock it up! At some point in the campaign, the staff will agree almost to a man that the candidate is a donkey—"Oh, what we could do with a really good candidate." And the candidate will lament to his intimates that the election could be his if only he had an efficient staff.

The split personality of the campaign may make some people uncomfortable, but it must be maintained. If egos are bruised, the candidate should not be the bruiser. If the campaign workers in Mudville blame the campaign manager for his pigheaded insistence on an extra day in Podunk, they will still work their tails off for the candidate. If the reporters at the *Blade* blame the press agent for an incompetent release they will still urge editorial endorsement of the candidate. If the fired office manager blames the campaign manager for his misfortune, he will still tell his friends to vote for Jones. Most importantly, the candidate must be saved from the temptation to work exclusively with his own kind. It is easier to get bogged down in a four-hour discussion among friends on what to do than it is actually to do it, more fun to plan a schedule of shopping center tours than actually to walk around shaking hands.

This does not mean that the candidate should not know what is going on and should not be ultimately responsible for the activities conducted in his name. Nor does it mean that campaigns should be organized on principles adopted from the Prussian Army. A high degree of internal democracy is good and necessary for morale. Campaign workers must be able to see and talk with the candidate from time to time. At least once a week, staff meetings, informal social events, and strategy sessions should be planned to involve as many volunteer workers as possible. But the lines of responsibility must be clearly defined.

WORKING WITH OTHER GROUPS

A major organizational problem of any campaign arises as it attempts to define its relations with other organizations. In order to be successful, campaigns must not only add members to their own organization, but also activate other organizations. The members of these other organizations may be only peripherally interested in the campaign, their alliance with it temporary, opportunistic, faint-hearted. "With all the good will in the world," as Michael Walzer puts it,

> cooperation is not easy, and in practice one must make do with considerably less good will than that. The crucial problem is that different organizations compete with one another. They find themselves fighting for a limited supply of members, money, media coverage, and so on. . . .

For all this, alliances and coalitions are possible and necessary. The familiar maxim about strange bedfellows is, in fact, an injunction: it is the aim of political action, of day-to-day argument and maneuver, to get people into the same bed who never imagined they could take a peaceful walk together.[6]

These problems are particularly pronounced in trying to deal with other campaigns. Off-year congressional candidates do not have to worry about the presidential campaign workers, but they do have to worry about senators and dog-catchers, local officials, and party regulars. And these relations may frequently be strained.

Many people tend to regard the process of a coalition building as one which involves explicit bargains and trade-offs. As John Kingdon notes.

The following sort of statement has come to be a commonplace in writings on campaigning: "Candidate X promised Y in order to get the support of voting bloc."[7]

As Kingdon and others have found, however, this kind of straight guid-pro-quo bargain is almost never struck.

Coalition members may very well receive rewards in the form of fulfillment of their policy or personal purposes for which they support the candidate. But the candidate will not tend to feel that he has paid any large cost in order to gain their support, because the things he feels they expect in return are regarded largely as simple continuations of his normal behavior.[8]

Or, as one Democrat put it in explaining his support from organized labor: "They just expect me to be a good liberal, and that's no burden at all. That's why I came here."[9]

Pseudo-sophisticated amateurs, in an effort to prove how worldly-wise they are, sometimes cause considerable embarrassment to their candidates, to the people they are approaching, and to themselves by assuming an unnecessarily Machiavellian posture: "All right, you guys, what do we have

to give you to get your support?" The need to avoid such
heavy-handed tactics doesn't mean that interest group leaders
shouldn't be cultivated, that they don't need to be asked
for their help, and that their needs don't need to be
accounted for in the campaign. Interest group leaders, in
one sense, want what everyone else wants from a campaign:
an assurance that your candidate is someone worth supporting. Where they differ from others is in a tendency to be
more issue-specific in their concerns. Labor leaders may
not give a damn about your candidate's foreign policy but
be very much concerned about situs picketing, secondary
boycotts, and the minimum wage. Peace group leaders may
care about foreign policy platforms and not give two hoots
about right-to-work problems. Gaining the support of an
interest group almost always requires the careful definition
of policy stands: you are dealing, after all, with someone
who knows his stuff. It can also involve the cultivation of
egos: groups leaders want assurances both that their concerns are important to you and that they themselves are
important. One way of helping to solve both problems at
the same time is to bring group leaders directly into the
campaign. Why should you do research on milk-marketing
quotas which the dairy association has already done and
would be flattered to be asked to provide?

How useful are group endorsements? There is considerable
disagreement on this question. Early studies of voting behavior placed considerable weight on the roles of opinion
leaders or "gatekeepers" in the flow of information to the
electorate. These gatekeepers, studies showed, tended to
process and direct the flow of information from the mass
media to the general public and thus much of what people
knew and thought about the candidates had been received
second hand. There is strong evidence today that television
has severely undermined the role of such opinion leaders,
at least in presidential campaigns. Because television is a
"low-effort" medium, candidates can use it to appeal di-

rectly to the people. Television now ranks as the most important source of political information by an overwhelming margin.

Using such findings, many students of campaigns argue that "new means of communication and the application of new technologies have caused a virtual revolution in campaigning. . . ."[10] Intermediary groups are less and less important as "candidates increasingly mobilize their own electorate" through direct appeals to mass publics.[11] But although the public's knowledge of Congress has increased, and although congressional candidates have begun increasingly to use TV, we suspect, and will argue further in Chapter 8, that the gatekeeper role retains considerable importance in congressional campaigns.

Endorsements, in and of themselves, mean little. If an endorsement means simply that Joe Blow will issue a press release in support of Charlie Candidate, it may have no significant effects at all. But if Charlie Candidate uses the endorsement effectively and if Joe Blow is willing to put his time where his mouth is, its effects can be significant.

Such endorsements may have the ripple effects of a stone thrown upon still waters. In 1972, for example, former White House aide Fred Bohen decided to enter the Democratic party primary for Congress in New Jersey's normally Republican 5th District. Two candidates were already in the race and had been campaigning for two months. Bohen, however, was able to secure the endorsement of Morris County Assemblywoman Ann Klein, the highest ranking Democratic officeholder in the district. He then sought the endorsement of former Democratic Governor Richard J. Hughes. Hughes checked with Klein. He then not only endorsed Bohen but agreed to hold a reception in his house featuring former Attorney General Ramsey Clark. Democratic leaders from throughout the district were invited. Attracted largely out of respect for Hughes, most of them came, and by the end of the evening most had endorsed Bohen and agreed to work for his nomination. Bohen won the primary easily.

Endorsements are important, then, to the extent to which they become known to those who trust and respect the endorser. Klein's endorsement of Bohen was important because it got him to Hughes. Hughes's was important because the area's Democratic leaders trusted Hughes's judgment. Many of us are affected by such word-of-mouth opinions. If someone whose judgment you trust recommends a book or movie, that is a book or movie you pay attention to. Many people behave the same way politically.

These ripple effects tend to be stratified. In the above instance, Hughes was trusted by party officials who had worked with him before, but his endorsement probably had little impact on the primary electorate as a whole. Similarly, an important union leader might have considerable influence among labor's rank and file, but none at all among farmers. So the key to successful coalition building is the breadth of support an endorser can generate rather than his prominence with one group. It also depends to a considerable degree upon the willingness of the endorser to make his position known to his kind of people.

One useful device for maximizing the effects of endorsements by individuals is the creation of special campaign groups such as "Lawyers for Jones," "Scientists and Engineers for Johnson," "Students for Smith." Here one capitalizes in part on the tendency of people to trust their own kind: students are more likely to listen to fellow students and lawyers to fellow lawyers than they are to listen to unknown campaign activists. Special groups such as these provide, moreover, a means of dispersing status and titles among large numbers of people. There can be only one campaign chairman and one municipal co-ordinator in each town, but the number of people who can be asked to serve as chairmen of special groups is practically without limit.

Relations of your man's campaign with those of other can-

didates and with the regular party organizations are particularly sensitive problems that must be dealt with largely by
ear. There just aren't any good rules that can be set forth to
explain how you deal with a situation in which the Democratic candidate for Congress is a "limp-wristed-commie-per-
missive-pinko" and his running mate for state office is a
"fascist-war-mongering-pig." As a general rule, it is probably
safe to say that the candidate of the same party as yours is
—despite his faults—better than his opponent, thus leaving
open the possibility of co-operation, if not necessarily working together. The regular organization, however, is another
problem entirely. It doesn't take long to discover the weak
links in the organizational chain. Some of its most trusted
district lieutenants, you will find, are so much out of touch
with their electorate as to defy explanation. Yet to send in
your own canvassers may alienate the district leader and his
remaining band of followers.

The problems with the party regulars can be very delicate.
Other things being equal, it is far better to have someone
who is known in the area and who knows the people in the
district do your door-to-door work. In "maximum-security"
high-rise apartments in urban areas this may be essential; it is
certainly desirable in older, well-established neighborhoods.
But the problem with relying on the old-timers is that
familiarity often breeds complacency and sloth. It is an
expected bit of political hyperbole for district leaders to
give elaborate assurances as to how well their areas are being worked: "Yeah, I got forty-three block workers out there
waiting the word to hit the streets. Don't worry about the
old Second Ward." That these forty-three workers were
conjured up as our peerless leader dozed through a late,
late show rerun of *The Last Hurrah* does not alter his
faith in their real existence, but from your perspective such
apparitions may prove less than effective. The old-time district leader probably does have thirty or forty back-pocket
votes: people who through the years have learned to trust

his judgment and who will vote or not vote as he suggests on Election Day. At the same time, there are probably fifty or sixty potential converts or non-voters whom he has written off. "Oh, don't bother with that house, they've never been for our side" or "Those folks are too new to the area to know what's going on" are statements that cannot always be accepted at face value.

There are a number of differences between amateurs and professionals that add to the difficulties of forming working alliances with regular party organizations. As James Wilson shows, differences of social class and of orientations toward issues and politics in general tend to divide the two groups. Moreover,

> Amateur clubs are committed to supporting the party but the enthusiasm with which their volunteer members work at getting out the vote is directly proportional to the perceived virtues of the candidates themselves. The regular organization, on the other hand, nominates candidates for a variety of reasons, and quality is only one of these (although one not neglected as frequently as some suggest). Making up the party ticket is a crucial factor in maintaining the regular organization, just as the quality or candidates is crucial for maintaining the amateur organization.[12]

Both groups obviously have much to gain from co-operation and are, in a sense, working toward the same end; but the tensions are nonetheless likely to surface at some point in the campaign.

LAUNCHING THE CAMPAIGN

"Every campaign starts too late" a statement you will understand best during the last week of yours. From a public perspective, congressional campaigns are quite short, lasting for perhaps five or six weeks. Press releases sent out earlier have little chance of being printed and advertising money spent that far in advance of election day is wasted. But the invisible, behind-the-scenes work that should precede the public part of the campaign has a major effect on how effectively a candidate's image and perspective comes across. It is difficult to get people thinking seriously about a November election before Labor Day, but Labor Day is too late even from a purely mechanical perspective. Take, for example, the problem of brochures. Most printers, you will find, want at least three weeks to produce any type of decent-looking work. Assuming that you can throw something together in a week, a Labor Day start means that your brochure won't be ready until four weeks before the election. Crude mimeographed fliers will have to do during the registration drive (see Chapter 5), at early shopping-center tours, at your first big fund-raising events. To paraphrase Noël Coward, mad dogs, Englishmen, and losers bask in the August sun.

The most important reason for an early start, however, is the need to plan and organize the strategy of your campaign. Even if adjustments must later be made, you should plan in advance as much detail as possible every step of the way. Day-to-day events are likely to prove so overwhelming in the final weeks as to leave no time or inclination for thinking big. Particularly important is the problem of maintaining perspective, a commodity that is always in short supply during the heat of battle. Candidates and their staffs seem to alternate between unjustified feelings of euphoria and what Jerry Bruno calls the "Grand Clong."[13] These feelings can seriously distort logic and literally destroy a campaign, unless a basic perspective on winning issues is settled on at the start of a campaign.

A classic example of such distortion was the campaign of Republican Wayne Dumont, Jr., for governor of New Jersey in 1965. Dumont's polls showed that incumbent Governor Hughes was extremely vulnerable on the issue of taxation, an issue which Dumont, rightly, hit hard in the early weeks of his campaign. About the same time, however, a professor of history at Rutgers University, Eugene Genovese, made a statement at an antiwar teach-in welcoming a Vietcong victory in Vietnam. Dumont seized on the event and called for the university to fire Genovese. At Republican rallies and American Legion meetings, the Genovese issue generated an electric response. People who sat and slept through Dumont's arguments on taxation leaped to their feet at the mention of Genovese. The polls showed, however, that most voters, particularly independents and Democrats, who Dumont had to win over, didn't give a damn what the good professor said but still cared about taxes. Buoyed by the cheers of his partisans, however, Dumont refused to believe the polls, dropped the tax issue, hit hard at Genovese, and lost decisively to Hughes on Election Day.

Dumont was a victim of what Hank Parkinson calls "candidate syndrome." "It is unbelievably difficult," he points out,

> to keep your perspective in a political campaign. Being human, you'll seek out the kind of counsel you want to listen to and ignore the warning signs that should alert you to the dangers of dead ends on the campaign trail. . . .
>
> Candidate syndrome can be beaten, but it takes monumental effort. It calls for the most difficult of all endeavors—realistic self-appraisal.[14]

Whether you are a movement or an individual, the first step in a campaign is to take stock of your own strengths and weaknesses, those of your opposition, and the ways in which they relate to the characteristics of the district. The candidate himself must, of course, play an important part in this process, and he must be absolutely candid. He must, moreover, be reminded frequently of this basic guide book to the campaign: "Keep it in a handy place and review it every week or so," Parkinson advises candidates. "During the final week of the campaign, study it at least once a day."[15] The advice applies to volunteers as well as to candidates. A good poll can be enormously helpful in devising strategic guidelines and in keeping the campaign's goals in focus. What a poll usually does, however, is simply to confirm what the objective views of savvy people would have indicated anyway. The essential problem is one of *objectivity*, and that is far easier to find in August than it is in October.

Another key step in planning campaign strategy is to decide on its basic theme.

> The purpose of the campaign theme is to simplify complex public issues into brief, clear, recognizable statements to the advantage of the candidate. . . . Election campaigns are fought not "on the issues" but on the themes.[16]

Remember that your campaign is competing with many others for the attention of the voter. The political competition is the least of your problem. You are up against thousands of commercial hucksters and summer attractions that are vying for the attention of the average citizen. To penetrate the fog of public indifference that envelops the political process takes repetition, catchiness, relevance, and all the imagination and ingenuity you can muster. To get through the indifference, your theme must be simple and must be repeated constantly. If the voter winds up knowing only one or two good things about your candidate, that is probably going to be one or two more things than he knows about your opponent. Thus, "the theme should run through all rallies, television performances, brochures, billboard ads, publicity releases, and other forms of communicating with the electorate."[17] Even the smallest details, if possible, should be tied in with the major theme: if you are emphasizing the vigor of the candidate, all pictures should show a man in motion; if ecology is a big issue, the bumper stickers should be green and all printing done on recycled paper.

In addition to planning strategy early in your campaign, there is the question of timing.

> The key to timing a major political contest successfully is acceleration. It doesn't really matter where the candidate

stands in the public affection at the start of a campaign.
What does matter is that the candidate gain some new
supporters every day.[18]

Since most voters don't even think about politics until the
last couple of weeks before the election, good timing often
means the exercise of restraint: save your big news stories
as long as you can, schedule your big events and rallies for
the last, bring in outside celebrities as close to Election Day
as you can, hold some of your key endorsements in your
back pocket.

Timing also means taking into account the characteristics of
the electorate. Voting studies have shown consistently that
the better informed the voter, the earlier he makes his decision on how to vote; the more interested he is in issues, the
sooner he begins to pay attention to the campaign. Those
who decide in the last two weeks are the least informed, the
least interested, and the most easily manipulated. This suggests a reversal of the usual process of dealing with issues.
Most candidates start simply, working for name recognition
and a project of the general theme. Only in the last few weeks
do they start publishing "white papers" and taking stands
on complex questions of public policy. The irony of this is
that those who are most likely to care about these kinds of
statements have already made up their minds by the time
they come out; those who are still undecided won't bother
reading a lengthy report. To prevent this situation, then, one
of the first things to be done in your campaign is to reverse
these tactics and prepare an elaborate issues book for use in
influencing elites and gaining the support (and money) of
opinion leaders.

The ideal campaign begins as long as a year before the
actual election. Before finally announcing one's candidacy,
this is a time for getting around the district, for getting to
know key people, for getting one's name associated with
"good" causes. The second step is to build an organization—
what Stephen Shadegg calls the basic cell group—a nucleus

of committed volunteers whose numbers, one hopes, will grad-ually expand. Two or three months before the filing deadline, the planning stage begins, and basic organizational responsibil-ities are determined. The next stage is the formal announce-ment of candidacy. It should come at least a few days be-fore the filing deadline, since the papers then will be crowded with similar releases. (It is best not to be too early because the earlier the announcement the less the audience.) The advantage of an early announcement is that may discourage others from filing. There is an old political adage that under-dogs file first, front-runners last; but it doesn't always hold.

Many books on campaigning give all sorts of hard-and-fast rules about the best times to do this and that, the best ways to accomplish what objectives. In the end, however, politics remains as much an art as a science. What is clear is the need to be objective, to keep the campaign simple and direct, and to involve as many people as possible in its opera-tions. The ultimate target is the undecided and uncommitted voter; but despite the growing importance of television, gate-keeping and opinion leaders can still be crucial. A good campaign is one that builds its activist base, that involves growing numbers of volunteers in significant roles. Whether they are party leaders, interest group leaders, or simply good friends, however, keeping your eye on the doughnut means remembering that the ultimate target is the voter: endorse-ments mean nothing until they are translated into votes.

NOTES

1. David A. Leuthold, *Electioneering in a Democracy* (New York: Wiley, 1968), p. 24.
2. Dick Simpson, *Winning Elections* (Chicago: Swallow Press, 1972), p. 35.
3. Ibid., p. 33.
4. For a detailed discussion of computer applications to campaigns, see Robert L. Chartrand, *Computers and*

Political Campaigns (Washington, D.C., Spartan Books, 1972).

5. Both the Republican and Democratic National Committees can supply candidates for Congress with assistance in setting up data processing systems and with lists based on census data, voting behavior, etc. This help, however, is available only to those who have already won nomination or have no primary election contests to contend with.

6. Michael Walzer, *Political Action: A Practical Guide to Movement Politics* (Chicago: Quadrangle Books, 1971), p. 40.

7. John Kingdon, *Candidates for Office* (New York: Random House, 1966), p. 62.

8. Ibid., p. 65–66.

9. Ibid., p. 63.

10. Robert Agranoff, *The New Style in Election Campaigns* (Boston: Holbrook Press, 1972), p. 6.

11. Frank J. Sorauf, *Political Parties in the American System* (Boston: Little, Brown, 1964), p. 108.

12. James Q. Wilson, *The Amateur Democrat* (Chicago: University of Chicago Press, 1962) p. 309.

13. "Grand Clong, a term I first heard from Frank Mankiewicz, is a common political disease, occurring when things get hopelessly loused up and you suddenly feel a rush of shit to the heart." Jerry Bruno and Jeff Greenfield, *The Advance Man* (New York: Morrow, 1971), p. 52.

14. Hank Parkinson, *Winning Your Campaign* (Englewood Cliffs, N.J., Prentice-Hall, 1970), p. 29.

15. Ibid., p. 39–40.

16. Dan Nimmo, *The Political Persuaders* (Englewood Cliffs, N.J., Prentice-Hall, 1970), pp. 54, 55.

17. Ibid., p. 54.

18. Stephen C. Shadegg, *The New How to Win an Election* (New York: Taplinger, 1964), p. 65.

CHAPTER 5

ADDING NEW VOTERS TO THE ROLLS

Textbooks teach us to regard voting as an important privilege of a democracy. Nonvoting is deplored as an abdication of civic responsibility. However, voting participation rates of Americans are often cited as being woefully behind those of other large democracies.

Voting turnout figures published by the Census Bureau highlight the disparity between citizen interest in democratic theory and voter apathy at the polls. In the 1968 presidential elections some 40 per cent of Americans eligible to vote did not avail themselves of their right to do so. In 1972 only 55 per cent of those eligible voted—the lowest percentage since 1948.

A major reason for the low percentage in 1972 was the addition of an estimated 25 million first time voters in the eighteen-to-twenty-one-age category. Despite optimistic early predictions, large numbers of this age group remained non-voters.

Most discussions of voter participation use the Census Bureau's formula for arriving at its figures. The Bureau calculates voter participation rates in the population by

dividing the number of persons actually voting by the total
number of persons of voting age.

Such figures can be somewhat deceiving. They do not take
into account the various state prerequisites besides age which
citizens must satisfy in order to be eligible to vote. For example, studies have estimated that from 15 to 12 per cent of
eligible voters are barred from registering because they
have moved and cannot meet residency requirements.[1]

Of the 35 million persons of voting age who reported that
they did not vote in 1968, 77 per cent reported that they
were not registered. Of those who were registered *91 per
cent voted*. Thus American turnout rates in terms of the
proportion of those *registered* who actually vote are comparable to turnout rates in Great Britain, West Germany,
France, and Canada—all of which have automatic registration systems.[2]

These figures have a practical political importance. They
mean that the name of the game is voter registration. One
noted student of voting has observed that "the act of registration itself requires as much if not more effort than the act of
voting once registration is secured."[3] Obviously, then, there is
no more important, and more often overlooked, part of most
campaigns than a good, solid voter registration drive.

The 1968 presidential election provides ample evidence of
the cruciality of voter registration. The election was very
close—Richard Nixon defeated Hubert Humphrey by 500,-
000 out of 73 million votes cast. As we pointed out above,
slightly more than the 26 million "eligibles" who did not vote
were not registered. Furthermore, a 1969 Gallup Poll showed
that two out of three unregistered people leaned toward the
Democrats. That represents about 18 million potential Democratic votes that were never cast in 1968—or about 17.5
million more votes than Humphrey lost by. As former Democratic National Chairman Lawrence F. O'Brien put it in dis-
cussing the importance of voter registration: "The presidential

election was lost by the Democratic party in the registration battlefield—not on the tube or in Chicago."[4]

Voter interest and participation are even lower in mid-term congressional elections. Voter registration drives and get-out-the-vote campaigns are even more important in these elections.

A number of social scientists have identified the demographic characteristics of the people who are least likely to vote. Most agree in listing the young, blacks, the poor, the less well educated, women, and people in rural areas.[5] From a practical perspective, a list like this one helps to identify target groups in conducting a registration drive. Answers to the question *why* people don't vote, however, are probably more important in a successful drive than knowing *who* doesn't vote.

It is clear, then, that few volunteer activities could be more important in marginal districts than adding new voters to the rolls. But before going into specific details of how to do it, we shall try to explain why so many Americans do not exercise their right to vote, to prepare the volunteer activist for contact with the apathetic by explaining some possible motivating factors.

A COST-GAINS CALCULUS OF VOTING

Anthony Downs has suggested that "every rational man decides to vote just as he makes all other decisions: if the returns outweigh the costs, he votes, if not, he abstains."[6] Whether or not you consider the typical non-voter a "rational man," this assumption provides a useful starting point for an analysis of non-voting.

Let us look first at the "costs" of voting. In every state but North Dakota and Alaska the act of voting must be preceded by the act of registering. In some parts of the country this task is confusing, difficult, and time consuming. When, for example, the registration office is open only on weekdays from 9 to 4, registering means taking time off from work for the average citizen. When inadequate facilities are provided registering may mean substantial personal inconvenience. As one New York City resident said in 1964, "I sure do want to vote against that man [Barry Goldwater], but I don't think I hate him enough to stand on that line all day long."

Time is the most obvious cost of voting. In low-income areas, however, many residents see the costs in more tangible terms. One of the most difficult jobs of registering voters in such neighborhoods is convincing people that registration does not subject them to new taxes, new debt obligations, or other financial responsibilities. Remember that people in these areas are likely to be highly suspicious of contacts with government.

Voting rates are lowest among the youngest age group (eighteen to twenty-five). There are a number of reasons for this. One factor closely associated with political participation is an individual's strength of partisan identification, and the strongest partisans participate the most. Young people, however, are not securely bound to the existing party system; they are less likely to evaluate political objects in party terms and less effectively involved in party fortunes than older citizens.[7] Furthermore, the demands of young adulthood, like getting a job and raising a family, reduce the time and attention one can spend on politics. In addition, as the most mobile age group in the population they face more legal barriers to voting than any other age group and often several times in a brief span of years.[8]

The much heralded "youth vote," as noted above, did not materialize in the 1972 presidential elections. Millions of young people failed to vote because many candidates failed to expend the effort in the systematic fashion necessary to register them. As a group continually replenished, as year after year more eighteen-year-olds come into the electorate, it can only be ignored by candidates at their peril. Youth

rst-time voters still constitute one of the great untapped
esources of electoral politics.

Downs's cost-gains theory of non-voting gets considerable
upport in a study by Stanley Kelley, Richard Ayres, and
Villiam Bowen. Kelley and his colleagues found that "local
ifferences in the turnout for elections are to a large extent
elated to local differences in the rules governing, and ar-
angements for handling, the registration of voters."[9] The
nore difficult it is to register, in other words, the higher the
roportion of non-voters.

Laws that make it difficult to register and to vote are par-
cularly intimidating to those with the least education.
Vhere the "costs" of voting are highest, differences in turn-
ut between low- and high-education groups are greatest.
'his suggests that the poorly educated may frequently be
on-voters partly because they are unaware of or intimidated
y the procedures necessary to register.

Insofar as some kind of cost-gains calculus can be used to
xplain non-voting, the goals of a registration drive should
early be:

1. To lower the "costs" of voting by making it as physi-
    cally and emotionally easy as possible for those eligible
    to register and vote.

2. To increase the perceived benefits by convincing poten-
    tial voters of the importance to *them* of the impending
    electoral contests.

We shall return to specific suggestions along these lines
ter in this chapter.

ON-VOTING AND SOCIAL PRESSURE

Not all decisions to vote or not to vote are based on rational
alculations. Even in Australia, where registration is auto-

matic and non-voters must pay a fine, 3 or 4 per cent of
those eligible do not vote. Morris Rosenberg, in a fascinating
series of interviews, found that political apathy in America
was related to various forms of social pressure. Some non-
voters, for example, viewed involvement in the political
process as a potential threat to more important social relationships. Lack of involvement was explained in ways like these:

> Right now I want to avoid friction—we were just married
> last June—so we try not to get into political discussions.

> I think it's better to do something that has direct results.
> . . . [In politics] you don't get any direct results. In
> Girl Scouts, you see the results; you have a chance to
> shape the character of the girls. I think that's more im-
> portant.

> People like to be entertained . . . and get away from the
> troubles of the day; and if you get them to start worry-
> ing about England and France and everything else in
> the world, they're just not interested.[10]

In trying to register voters, you will probably encounter
some who will actively resist even the suggestion of involvement. Some radicals, some alienated individuals, quite a few
who find politics too dull and uninteresting to merit their attention may never be brought to the polls.

The United States is not a very political nation. Few
Americans are active in politics, and for most, deciding to
vote or not vote is a relatively trivial matter. It is your job
to make the decision to vote less trivial. Nothing, of course
can substitute for a good candidate and an exciting campaign
to motivate the normally apathetic; but in many instances
candidates and campaigns are too remote from people's every
day experience to serve as catalysts to action. The key to
voter registration is often social pressure. People vote because
they are embarrassed not to, because their neighbors do, be
cause it is accepted as one of the duties of a loyal American
or simply because someone asks them to. One reason that

upper- and middle-income citizens are more likely to vote than the poor is that social pressures encouraging voting are much stronger in more affluent communities. Successful voter registration drives often depend, therefore, on successful inter-personal contacts. This is one reason for preferring the door-to-door campaign to telephone contacts.

REGISTRATION STRATEGIES
AND ELECTORAL SUCCESS

Something in the democratic spirit is satisfied when a new voter is brought to the polls. Realistically speaking, how-ever, altruism and democratic ideals have little to do with effective registration drives. "The candidate who is deadly serious about winning," Lawrence O'Brien wrote in the Demo-cratic campaign manual for 1964, "is always concerned about registration." Or, as Ern Reynolds told the participants at a Republican campaign management seminar in 1966, voter registration is "a strategic maneuver. . . . The non-regis-trants represent the unsold market, the people who have not been reached. These unregistered people represent power waiting to be seized."

The registration drive is the opening gun of the public phase of an effective campaign. No matter how thoroughly the job has been done before, it must be done again. Be-tween 1972 and 1974, eight million Americans turned eight-een. Almost forty million eligible voters moved and must re-gister. In every congressional district in the country, there are, right now, anywhere between 40,000 and 100,000 eligible voters who are not properly registered. The key to unlocking the doors of these enormous reserves of untapped vote power is selectivity. In an effective registration drive we follow Rule 3 as explained in Chapter 1: hunt ducks where the ducks are; and we add a corollary: hunt ducks, not crows. If you are a Democrat, in other words, your goal is to register Democrats not Republicans.

Thus the first step in a voter registration drive is *targeting*. The object of "targeting" is to ensure that the campaign's resources—almost always limited—can be allocated to achieve their maximum effectiveness. Before beginning any registration operations you should rank all the precincts in your district according to the return that can be expected from the voter registration drive. You are looking for precincts that are heavily in favor of your candidate or his party with a low proportion of residents registered to vote. Two other factors to consider in picking your target precinct are population density and geographical compactness. The denser and the smaller a precinct is, the easier it is to work in.

From these factors an "index of registration priority" can be created, with each precinct in the district ranked from best through worst in terms of its probable yield in a voter registration drive. If someone on the campaign staff cannot construct such an index, a political scientist, sociologist, or statistician at a local college can often be recruited to help.

With this index, you should be able to identify those precincts which are heavily in favor of your party but are underregistered.

The logic of this is simply that most people—particularly those of low partisan loyalties—are likely to vote as their neighbors do. Most non-voters do not have strong attachments to either party, and though lacking such commitments and both interest in and knowledge of public affairs, they may be susceptible to social pressure. If they live in Democratic neighborhoods, these pressures are likely to be Democratic, and in Republican areas, Republican.

The specific tactics used in a voter registration drive must be shaped to accord with state and local laws and practices. In many states, for example, any individual passing a test and meeting certain qualifications can be deputized to register voters. In these states you should get as many of your canvassers deputized as possible so they can register new voters on the spot. Other states send special mobile units into each neighborhood or town for extra evening hours of registration. Here the canvassing teams should be prepared to take new voters directly to the mobile unit.

A deputy registrar cannot, of course, refuse to register a citizen on partisan grounds. But the job of the registration canvasser is to increase his candidate's edge, and where special efforts are required to get people registered, those efforts should not be wasted on non-voters you believe may vote for the opposition. In those states which do not allow deputies or mobile registrations, the task is a difficult one that may involve repeated call-backs. It involves hard work and meticulous attention to details. People identified as non-voters must often be recontacted repeatedly and sometimes literally carried to the place of registration. All of this is tedious and often frustrating work involving more determination and tenacity than brain power. But if well executed, out of such "donkey work" can come victory for your candidate.

If manpower is limited—and it usually is—lists of registered voters can be compared with city directories, jury lists, electric company lists, or reverse-order phone books that classify householders by street addresses. Registration goals can then be set and canvassers sent to specific households which are known to contain unregistered people. These lists, however, are seldom up to date or complete and should be substituted for door-to-door campaigns only as a last resort. A registration canvass can also be conducted by phone.

Whatever the method chosen, a useful organizational device is to set a quota for each canvasser. Experience shows that twenty is a reasonable number. To the ambitious, this may sound low, but with call-backs, reminders, and transportation figured in, one canvasser will find it very difficult to be responsible for more than about twenty. Canvassers who work quickly can always be given a second list to cover in another district. Teams of two—preferably male and female—are most effective in door-to-door campaigns. In non-English-speaking districts, one of each pair should speak the other language.

It is always wise in a political campaign to establish liaison with other groups that may share your goals. The League of Women Voters, which is non-partisan, can be very helpful in providing research help on local laws and volunteers to work in certain districts. Labor unions are often active in registration work.

Most important is contact with the regular party organization, as district leaders are supposed to be familiar with every resident of their districts. Your first stop should be at the leader's home to check your list of potential registerees against his knowledge. But remember that by suggesting that the district may contain unregistered members of his party, you are implicitly criticizing his performance as a party leader. Tact and diplomacy may prove useful, but you should never lose sight of your goal of enrolling new voters.

Volunteer canvassers must be thoroughly briefed before they go out to register potential voters. Each one should know the election laws upside down and backward and explain them carefully. Nothing is more annoying to the potential voter than traveling to the registration office only to find that he cannot produce some proof of age or naturalization or whatever else the state law may require that the canvasser forgot to tell him about. Handbills or cards that list important laws, give times and places of registration, and provide a phone contact for further information should be carried by each canvasser. Volunteer headquarters should also provide back-up support for canvassers in the form of transportation and baby-sitting pools and access to legal counsel if called for.

In the next chapter we will discuss the election canvass. It is often impossible in terms of funds, volunteers, and time to mount two door-to-door canvasses in the same campaign. Often a candidate must revert to a telephone canvass for the registration drive or combine the two drives in one single operation.

Door-to-door canvassing, however, is by far the preferable

method and generally worth added manpower costs. This is true, first, because of the growing trend toward the use of unlisted phones. (In New York City, for example, one subscriber in four has an unlisted number.) Twenty per cent of the total nationwide population, moreover, has no phone. Second, direct personal contact is more effective. Studies show that it is "much easier to refuse over the phone than it is to refuse a request in face-to-face situations; and that the not-at-homes are apparently not reduced appreciably by the phone call, which would be its main justification."[11]

In contacting voters, whether by phone or in person, the goals of the canvasser are to lessen the perceived costs of voting and to increase the perceived benefits. Lessening the costs means making it as convenient as the law allows to register and vote. Offers to provide baby-sitters and transportation will lower the costs of voters. For many, getting information is one of the costs that can be reduced or eliminated; you can save these citizens the time and effort of finding out whether or not they are eligible, where and when they can register, and so on. Increasing the perceived benefits means relating the upcoming election to candidates or issues that are important to the individual in question. Social pressure may also be used as a motivating appeal—"Tomorrow," you might say, "I'm taking your neighbors the Smiths to the registrar. May I take you too?"

APPROACHING THE NON-VOTER

Before any doorbells are rung, the campaign organization should have identified target precincts and set quotas. It should have established liaison with other groups working on registration to avoid duplication of effort. It should have thoroughly briefed each volunteer. It should have acquired legal counsel and have contact with volunteers for baby-sitting and transporting potential voters to the registrar. It should have provided each volunteer with campaign brochures, cards, or throw-aways outlining local laws, "hard cards" for recording information (these are described in greater detail in Chapter 6), a map of the district to be covered, a list of registered and unregistered citizens in the district, application forms for absentee ballots, change-of-address cards, and a clipboard for holding everything together.

When you, the volunteer, approach your target it goes without saying that you should be neat in appearance and dressed appropriately for your surroundings. You should, of course, be courteous, patient, well informed, but not patronizing. You should know what you're talking about.

Market research clearly indicates that the natural approach is best; People are quick to spot a put-on or set speech. Each volunteer will, with practice, develop his or her own particular line of attack. Role-playing sessions, in which volunteers alternate playing the parts of canvasser and of, say, newly transplanted voters, radicals who don't believe in working within the system, or new voters who know nothing about registration laws or the impending elections, are useful warm-ups, but no substitute for on-the-job experience.

You might use as a basic guide the following interview outline adapted from a Democratic party campaign manual; it can be used by workers for any party with appropriate changes.

Before you set out, using the map and registry list, plan your itinerary. Fill out the names, addresses, and phone numbers on "hard cards" for each household you plan to visit.

When you call on a family or visit them, be as brief as possible. Limit your talk to something like the following:

1. "Hello, is this Mrs. Daylene Burnside?"
2. "Mrs. Burnside, I'm Pete Weaver from the Steve Alinikoff-for-Congress Committee. I'm doing some volunteer work for the Alinikoff-for-Congress campaign.

We're trying to get in touch with all the Democrats in this neighborhood. Do you have a moment?" If she says no, thank her and ask when you may call back later.

3. If she says yes, say, "Would you mind telling me if you are a Republican or a Democrat?"

   A. If she says Republican, mark an "R" on the hard card and go on to questions 4 and 5.

   B. If she says Democrat, mark a "D" and go on to question 6.

   C. If she says independent, ask, "Do you think yourself closer to the Democratic or Republican party most of the time?" If she says Democratic, mark the card "ID" and go on to question 6. If she says neither, leave the "I" to stand alone. If she says Republican, mark the card "IR" and go to questions 4 and 5.

4. This question is for Republicans and independent Republicans only: "Are there any other people eighteen or over in your house?"

5. (This question too is only for those leaning toward the opposite party) "Are any of them Democrats?" If there are, ask their names, write them down, and find out how you can get in touch with them. Terminate the interview with a courteous good-by.

6. If the answer to question 3 is Democrat or leaning Democratic, ask, "May I have your full name? Phone number?" Write these down or correct any errors on your card.

7. Since Mrs. Burnside's name is not on your registry list, ask if you can provide assistance in registering. Frequently a voter who is not on the registry list will insist that he or she is in fact registered. Sometimes this is because the registry lists are not up to date, so ask when the voter registered. More often it is because the voter has moved or been purged from the rolls. Asking "When did you last vote from this ad-

dress?" will usually elicit the necessary information. If Mrs. Burnside hasn't voted in two years (four in some states, one in others) or has moved since voting, consult your registration information card and tell her if she has to register again or file change of address notice.

These seven questions are part of any registration canvass. The following five questions, while not specifically related to a registration campaign, can provide essential information which is best obtained at this time. By identifying and locating absentee voters, for example, one has the time to send off application forms and reminders to vote to students, servicemen, and others who are out of state.

8. Ask, "Are there any other eligible voters in your house? Anyone about to turn eighteen?" If the answer is yes, list each name on your form. Then ask questions 6 and 7 and enter the replies. Note that roomers or relatives may have separate phones.

9. "Does any member of your household who is eligible to vote happen to be in the armed services or away from home in school or on a job or in a hospital? Will anyone be away on election day?"

10. If the answer is yes, ask, "May I give you [or send] a request form for an absentee ballot?" This can be very important. An average of twenty or thirty persons in each election district in the country who are eligible to vote absentee do not. One reason is that the deadline for applying is often so far in advance of the election that most people simply forget. Just as the absentee vote swung California to Richard Nixon in 1960, they may well provide a margin of victory in many races. There are few better opportunities for picking up sure votes for your candidate than the careful distribution of absentees forms.

11. If Mrs. Burnside seems quite interested, ask, "Would

you be willing to put in a few hours a week on volunteer work for the party, as I am doing? Can you do phoning from your home? Would you be willing to host a coffee for our candidate?" Record this information carefully and be sure to call back if she expresses an interest. No volunteer can be as effective as one who actually lives in the neighborhood.

12. End the interview, saying, "Thank you very much, Mrs. Burnside. We will add your name, if you don't mind, to our mailing lists, and would appreciate your talking to your neighbors about the _____ campaign. Good-by."

If you are working for a Republican candidate, of course, you must vary this procedure accordingly. If you are working for an individual candidate rather than the entire party ticket, you may want to ask questions which refer specifically to support for that candidate. In a registration canvass, however, the strictly partisan approach is probably best. In off-year elections most voters vote the straight ticket. More important, they are more likely to have some notion of what the party label means than they are to have heard anything about an individual candidate.

FOLLOWING THROUGH AFTER REGISTRATION

The registration drive is the opening gun of the door-to-door campaign. It is not an isolated exercise in good citizenship, but an integral part of any effective election strategy. It has two goals: registering new voters and compiling information for later activities. In this second aspect it overlaps with the canvassing guidelines described in Chapter 6, many of which also apply to registration. Any bits of information acquired in registering new voters should be carefully recorded for future use.

The registration drive also serves as a shake-down cruise

for the volunteer staff. It is a good place to spot weaknesses in the organization and it serves to initiate the volunteer in the art of canvassing. If it is to be effective, it must be carefully planned. To reduce the costs of voting, volunteers must know the election laws.

They must be backed up by transportation and baby-sitting pools. To increase the perceived benefits of voting, volunteers must know the area, the issues and the candidates. And there must be follow-through: the information compiled by each volunteer must be carefully processed and recorded. Those who need absentee ballots should get them. Those who need transportation should get it. Those who agree to help should be contacted immediately. Once the registration deadline is past, you can't go back again. No matter how much someone may want to vote for your candidate, he cannot do so if he is not registered, and his vote multiplied through every precinct in the district may mark the margin between victory and defeat.

NOTES

1. Edward C. Dreyer and Walter A. Rosenbaum, *Political Opinion and Behavior: Essays and Studies,* 2nd ed. (Belmont, Calif.: Wadsworth, 1970), p. 405.
2. Ibid.., p. 181.
3. Philip E. Converse, with Richard Niemi, "Non-Voting Among Young Adults in the United States," in William J. Crotty, Donald M. Freeman, and Douglas S. Gatlin *Political Parties and Political Behavior,* 2nd ed. (Boston: Allyn & Bacon, 1971), p. 463.
4. Democratic National Committee, *Campaign '72: Voters' Registration Manual* (Washington, D.C.: 1972), p.1.
5. See Angus Campbell, et al., *The American Voter* (New York: Wiley, 1960).

6. Anthony Downs, *An Economic Theory of Democracy* (New York: Harper & Row, 1961), p. 123.

7. Campbell, et al., op. cit., p. 264.

8. Converse, with Niemi, op. cit., pp. 462–65.

9. Stanley Kelley, Jr., Richard E. Ayres, and William G. Bowen, "Registration and Voting: Putting First Things First," *American Political Science Review*, 61 (June 1967).

10. Morris Rosenberg, "Some Determinants of Political Apathy," *Public Opinion Quarterly*, 18 (Winter 1954–55).

11. G. Allen Brunner and Stephen J. Carroll, "The Effect of Prior Telephone Appointments on Completion Rates and Response Content," *Public Opinion Quarterly*, 31 (Winter 1967–68), pp. 652–54.

CHAPTER 6

WINNING VOTES

HOW THE AMERICAN VOTER DECIDES

Over the past three decades social scientists have produced a large amount of information concerning the voting habits of the American electorate.[1] This has been a major contribution to the development of a scientific study of politics which seeks to explain and predict, as well as describe, central political processes.

The studies are not only of academic interest but also offer many insights to the political activist with more practical political concerns.

Of major importance, according to these studies, is the concept of party identification:

Few factors are of greater importance in our national elections than the lasting attachment of tens of millions of Americans to one of the parties. These loyalties establish a major division of electoral strength within which the competition of particular campaigns takes place. And they are an important factor in insuring the stability of the party system itself.[2]

Although in terms of candidate preference, these partisan loyalties are not determinate, party identification serves to filter political information and organize a citizen's more short-run attitudes. It thus provides the element of continuity in American elections.

Voters do not evaluate parties and candidates in each election *de novo*. Rather,

> in a world where information is difficult to obtain and imperfect when obtained, partisan identity becomes an organizing precept enabling the citizen to behave consistently with his basic political predisposition without expending great efforts in either seeking information or reaching a voting decision.[3]

The voting decision itself can be seen as

> the interplay of candidate imagery, the low level of mass political information, the absence of strong ideologies and meaningful issues across a large segment of the electorate, and, primarily, long-term psychological commitments to political parties. . . .[4]

Political activists, no matter how enthusiastic they may be, can do little to affect the distribution of party identifiers in a constituency. And as partisan identification is long-term and relatively stable, large-scale shifts seldom occur and then usually as the result of some national crisis.[5] Activists should therefore avoid races where the "normal vote"—measured either by past election returns or a public opinion survey of partisan identification—is strongly against them.

Partisan identification rates also raise problems of campaign strategy. Nationally, about 45 per cent of the electorate identifies with the Democratic party and 25 per cent with the Republican; about 30 per cent are independents. These distributions dictate different strategies for the two parties. In order for the Democrats to win, they must reinforce their own voters and persuade about half of the independents to vote Democratic. On the other hand, for the Republicans to win, they must not only reinforce their own voters and persuade a large proportion of independents but also convert a significant group of normally Democratic voters.

Political interest and knowledge about candidates and issues are closely related to party identification. Both increase as the strength of party identification increases. The voting studies show that the picture of the independent voter as the most interested, most informed type of citizen, who casts his vote after carefully considering all the alternatives, is largely a myth. In fact, they are often the least interested and least informed. They also are the most easily swayed and tend to swing back and forth between the parties.

Another important factor in elections is the differing defection rates of partisan identifiers. The more an individual identifies with a political party, the less likely he is to vote for the opposite party. It has also been found that both strong and weak Republican identifiers are less likely to desert their party than their Democratic counterparts. Thus, a Democratic candidate in a district with a partisan identification distribution which forces him to seek a large number of normally Republican votes will probably have less chance of winning than a Republican in a district with an equivalent but opposite party identification distribution.

The voting studies have brought out another factor of the electoral decision upon which activists can have some effect. They have confirmed what many politicians have known for some time—that most people have little interest in or knowledge about politics. Most have only a surface familiarity with the "major issues of the day" and have little information about the policy positions of candidates. In fact, large numbers know nothing at all about candidates for Congress—not even their names. This creates a situation in which many voters seem to vote in a non-rational way, unrelated to the issues.

The issues which seem very important to political scientists or newspaper pundits may not seem so important to the man in the street. Or he may perceive little difference in the candidates' respective positions on certain issues. This general ignorance about candidates and issues offers a fertile field for volunteer activists. An effective door-to-door canvass can uncover the issues that really count with the average voter. Most often they are tied up with the voter's family, job, and immediate life situation. When asked what problem most concerns them, many voters will automatically respond pollution, peace, or some other world problem. Further probing, however, generally reveals that what they are in fact most worried about may be rising food prices, crime in the streets, or busing their children to a school outside their neighborhood. While the Vietnam war was a burning moral issue on American college campuses for over a decade, it did not become important to the general American public until large numbers of American men began to get killed or captured there.[6]

By discovering what issues are *really* important to voters in a constituency and what voters want to see done about them, volunteers can provide extremely useful political intelligence to their candidate and his campaign. Moreover, volunteers can recontact voters with information about the candidate's position on those issues.[7]

Several recent studies have shown that voters will vote "rationally" when they know the positions of the candidates on the issues *most important to them* and can perceive *differences* between the two candidates on such issues. The task of getting such information to the voter falls mainly on volunteers who are willing to do the hard but essential work of personal contact at the grass-roots level.

THE DOOR-TO-DOOR CANVASS

For many years reformers have attacked machine politics with its attendant graft, corruption, and patronage abuses.

In many parts of the country once-powerful machines have
been overthrown by dedicated amateurs. In other areas they
have crumbled and decayed from within; out of touch with
social change, insensitive to the demands of the New Politics,
and unable to build new bases of support, the boss-ruled
machine has become a political anachronism. In their zeal
for displacing boss rule, however, some reform groups have
thrown the baby out with the bath water. They have destroyed the machines, and along with them, some of the most
legitimately effective techniques of political activity yet ad-
vised.

One of these techniques—the systematically organized and
co-ordinated door-to-door canvass—has increasingly become
a vital part of New Politics campaigns. The door-to-door
canvass, the purpose of which is to find, register (as we
have seen), and deliver sympathetic voters to the polls, has
been an effective staple of practical political action for at least
140 years. In 1840 Abraham Lincoln urged his party, the
Whigs, to

> organize the whole state, so that every Whig can be
> brought to the polls . . . divide the county into small
> districts and appoint in each a sub-committee . . . make
> a perfect list of voters and ascertain with certainty for
> whom they will vote . . . and on Election Day see that
> every Whig is brought to the polls.[8]

This technique of finding, registering, and bringing your
supporters to the polls has been used successfully by machine
politicians for generations. Progressives, however, have seldom
employed careful, precinct-by-precinct organization. Even
the McCarthy campaign of 1968, while very effective in
door-to-door activities, was only infrequently organized at
the precinct level in such a way as to make maximum use
of the canvass.

The reasons for this neglect of such an important electoral

tool are probably connected with the distaste many reformers have felt for the more cynical aspects of machine operations. However, there is no reason volunteers working for reform cannot be as effectively organized as ward-heelers receiving a political boss's patronage. Some elections are bought or stolen. Most, however, have been won by those forces possessing the largest sympathetic audience and the superior organization capable of mobilizing that audience and bringing it to the polls. Organization, not patronage, is the the key word. Often, if reformers had been organized as well or better than their opposition—tightly, all the way down to the precinct level—they would have won.

HOW TO ORGANIZE AN EFFECTIVE CANVASS

Efficient organization begins with the delineation of simple functional tasks, first within a particular geographic area. In order to facilitate the finding and bringing of sympathetic voters to the polls, subdivide the congressional district into smaller, more manageable units, usually the smallest electoral unit. By limiting the territory to be covered, you enhance local contact with the voter.

The precincts in the district should be "targeted" as in the registration drive, but on a somewhat different basis. For the election canvass you are particularly interested in two types of precincts: (1) those high in preference for your candidate but relatively low in voter turnout; and (2) those which have shown a high incidence of split tickets in particular elections or swings back and forth between parties and candidates from election to election.

Voter registration figures, previous election returns, and any polls which may be available can be used to construct indexes for the two types of precincts. When that is done, the precincts can be ranked from best to worst, with maximum effort to be expended on the high priority ones.

A different strategy is also called for each type of precinct. In the first you are interested in identifying, reinforcing, and mobilizing voters who probably already favor your candidate but who might not vote without outside encouragement.

In the second, "split-swing," precincts you are trying to identify, *persuade*, and mobilize voters who are undecided about whom to support. These voters are usually among the least-informed and least-educated in the district. In recent years, however, suburban areas in particular have produced a new breed of swing voters who are largely upper-middle class, well educated, well off, and *more* interested in issues than the average voter. A canvass in these precincts should attempt to discover what issues most concern them *and* what solutions they think the government should attempt. Information about your candidate's position on these issues should then be delivered to these voters as soon as possible. If time and manpower permit, they should be revisited for a final assessment of their attitudes toward the candidate before Election Day.

If a registration canvass has been carried out, you already have information on the party preference of your newly registered voters and of some other registered voters. This information forms the basis for the "hard card" file that is essential to effective precinct organization. Such a file contains a card for everyone eligible to vote in the precinct— registered or unregistered. You may devise a color scheme to denote voter preference and registration status. And, if resources permit, a separate set of punch cards can be made for computer use.

Hard card files should be kept in triplicate—one set by the congressional campaign headquarters and two by the precinct leader. Even where the central file is computerized, each precinct should have its own set of cards, one arranged alphabetically by voter's last name and the other by voter's street address. A sample of such a card is printed below.

                                     Town or
Address: _____ ward _____Precinct _____

Name: _____ Occupation: _____

Party preference: Phone: _____
   D   R   I

Needs: Can Contribute:

_____Absentee ballot   _____Financially
_____Baby sitter   _____HQ work
_____Transportation   _____Precinct work
_____Other   _____Poll watching
                                    _____Election Day phoning
                                    _____Other

Additional Info: (e.g., union member, civil servant, etc.;
                 likely to split ticket, will vote late in
                 day; other useful information)

Needs to be recontacted: YES   NO

Before setting up your own system, you will find it useful
to discover whether existing information sources are willing
to work with you. Some district leaders from the regular
organization may already have up-to-date files, and a great
deal of time can be saved if these people are willing to work
with volunteers.

Before any volunteers are sent into the field, the organization should be well prepared. No one should approach a voter
without having been thoroughly briefed on the nature of the
area he is covering, the key issues of the campaign, and information about the candidate. It is both embarrassing to the
volunteer and damaging to the campaign for its agents in the
field to be uninformed, misinformed, or naïve. Ideally, briefing sessions should be scheduled on a regular basis. If this is
impossible, volunteers can report to some central headquarters
before being sent into the field. If manpower permits, a chair-

man for each precinct or election district should be appointed to serve as a local link in the chain of command.

More important, don't send out any canvasser before making a thorough analysis of the district, aimed at locating target precincts and on going where the campaign is strongest in potential vote but weak in organization. The volunteer should be particularly careful not to attempt a do-it-yourself operation. Successful vote mobilization efforts depend upon careful and well-co-ordinated campaign strategies. Canvassers should not go into opposition strongholds—your chances of scoring converts are slim and may be more than offset by the number of opposition voters you draw to the polls. Marginal districts and districts which historically have displayed wide swings in voting behavior should receive particular attention. And it is the function of the campaign headquarters, not of the individual volunteer, to identify such districts.

When canvassers actually go into the field, they should go in pairs, if possible. Where a local precinct worker is already available, at least one other person (preferably of the opposite sex) should be sent in to help. Most people are more receptive to two women or to a man and a woman than they are to one or two strange men. Moreover, it is easier for two people to make a graceful exit from a difficult conversation than it is for a lone worker.

If the volunteer cannot get past the door, his time is wasted. Any tactics that lessen the suspicion of householders should be employed. This is why a clean-cut appearance, identifying buttons or even hats, decorated clipboards, and so forth, should be used. A neatly typed, signed letter of authorization or similarly impressive-looking credentials may be helpful in gaining entry to apartments with doormen, college dormitories, old age homes, etc.

Timing is also important. The best times to conduct a door-to-door canvass are evenings between 6:30 and 9:30, Saturdays from 11 A.M. until 5 P.M., and Sunday afternoons. More people are at home week nights than on Saturdays, but they are more likely to give a courteous hearing to canvassers on the weekend than they are at night. Where no one is home, the canvasser should note the time of the attempted contact so he can make his call-back at a different hour. If a registration canvass has already been conducted, assign volunteers for canvassing in the district where they worked for registration.

CONTACTING VOTERS

The objectives of a good canvass are twofold: *to gain information and to mobilize lukewarm supporters.* The principal job of the canvasser is not to argue issues with the voters, but to evaluate voters in terms of candidate preferences. The emphasis must be on mobilization, not conversion. Arguing issues with voters is bad politics for many reasons, and the costs in terms of wasted time which could be more profitably spent canvassing (evaluating) other voters are very high.

Several studies have shown that few voters are *converted* by visits from election workers. One such study employing survey data on presidential and congressional elections from 1952 to 1966, showed that canvassing had little effect on changing voters' preferences for national or local offices.[9] Our data (see Chapter 3) show significant preference effects, particularly among marginal voters whose partisan identifications are weak. But in off-year elections in particular, the turnout factor is more important. Arguments are not only a waste of time, but they can cause lackadaisical supporters of your opponent to become sufficiently angry to go out and vote.

"Score" or rate voters on a rating system approved by campaign headquarters. A simple 1-to-5 scale is often best. You rate those voters most favorable to your candidate as 1s, probably favorable as 2s, undecided as 3s, probably against as 4s, and definitely against as 5s. Those whom you have rated 2 and 3 should be contacted with follow-up visits to ascertain more clearly their candidate preference.

Record these ratings and any appropriate comments, such as the voters opinions on issues or his special interests, on canvassing sheets that list each resident of the precinct. Wait until you have left the voter's house before writing anything on the canvassing sheet. Later, transfer this information to the voter's hard card in the files. But be careful. Smiles and vaguenesses are readily granted and should not be mistaken for commitments. Statements like "Oh yes, Jones is a fine fellow" do not deserve 1s on the hard cards. Be suspicious.

As a canvasser, you must work hard to find out where people really stand; yet at the same time, you must avoid getting involved in long-winded discussions, even if friendly, unless the person is indicating a willingness to work. If so, by all means pin him down. Will he or she host a coffee klatsch? Make phone calls? Canvass? If affirmative, get the person's phone number and give it to the campaign manager.

As a canvasser, make yourself informed and read the candidate's literature carefully before you start out. Be prepared to answer questions about his stands on major issues, his background, his chances for election, and so on. If you cannot answer a question, don't guess. Get the person's phone number and promise to get back to him. Make a note of the query, get the answer from campaign headquarters, and call the person back. Even a well-informed canvasser might do well to refer some questions to headquarters, as these call-backs are easily made and indicate interest and concern.

Make your canvass questions subtle and unobtrusive. Indirect questions often elicit information best. But most important, do not argue—evaluate!

As an effective canvasser, you will do more than simply gather information. For many voters, you will be their only contact with the campaign. It is your job to sell the candidate. But "selling" in this context does not mean extended argument or debate: the soft sell is most effective.

Indeed, simply getting the voter to recognize the candidate's name is half the battle.

The University of Michigan's Survey Research Center's study of mid-term elections points up very dramatically the impact of name recognition on voting behavior.[10] The chances are excellent that any given voter will not have heard of either candidate (this was true of 59 per cent of those sampled). If he has heard of only one, the chances are two-to-one that it will be the incumbent. Suppose that you are working for a Democrat against the incumbent Republican.

Table V

Voter was aware of

Voted for candidate	Both candidates	Own party candidate only	Other party candidate only	Neither candidate
Of own party	83%	98%	60%	92%
Of other party	17	2	40	8
Total	100%	100%	100%	100%
	(N=196)	(N=166)	(N=68)	(N=368)

SOURCE: Donald E. Stokes and Warren E. Miller, "Party Government and the Saliency of Congress," in Angus Campbell, et al., *Elections and the Political Order* (New York: Wiley, 1966), p. 205.

The data in Table V suggest the following possible effects of simply impressing voters with the name of the Democratic challenger: for those voters who have heard of neither candidate, name recognition can increase the potential vote of Democratic voters from 92 per cent to 98 per cent and of

those who consider themselves Republicans from 8 per cent
to 40 per cent. Among Democrats who are familiar only with
the Republican incumbent, name recognition can increase
the Democrat's share from 60 per cent to 83 per cent. Even
among Republicans who know the name of the incumbent,
familiarity with the Democratic challenger can increase his
share of the vote from 2 per cent to 17 per cent.

What these figures suggest is simply that the issue content of the canvasser's appeal is far less important than con-
veying the most elementary facts: first, that an election is
about to take place, and second, that the name of one of
the candidates is the one you are working for. Never mention
your opponent by name. Mention your own candidate's
name as often as taste permits.

PUSH THE "BRAND NAME." Rule 1 of political campaigning
is not to get discouraged. One major source of discouragement for many volunteers is the incredibly high level of
public apathy and political ignorance. It is important to bear
constantly in mind the generally low level of importance even
today which the average citizen attributes to politics in
general and to Congress in particular. Political decisions are
low-priority decisions for most people—far less important, say,
than the decision to buy a new car.

One attribute of low-priority decisions is that they are
highly vulnerable to outside influence. Without meaning to
make any invidious comparisons, the voting decisions of
many citizens are in some ways comparable to their tooth-
paste-buying decisions. When the consumer needs toothpaste,
he goes to the store. His objective is to buy toothpaste:
what kind he buys is not important; the decision is a low-
priority one. The job of the Colgate company (and its ad
agency) is to intercept the consumer somewhere between his
home and the store with the name "Colgate." Since the brand-
name decision is trivial and since "Colgate" may be the only
name that rings a bell, chances are that he will buy Colgate.

The voter who gives politics a low priority is similarly in-
clined to choose the brand-name of the candidate that rings
some kind of bell. Canvassers can make those bells ring.

ELECTION DAY

The key to well-run Election Day activities is good organization and a well-thought-out battle plan. Several weeks before the election, the campaign manager should devise a clear
schedule of the needs and activities of Election Day. He maps
out clearly and in great detail what will be expected of
precinct workers, poll watchers, and all others involved in the
Election Day effort.

The first aspect of Election Day organization to consider
is whether to run a centralized or a decentralized operation.
There are advantages and disadvantages to both approaches
that have to be weighed in light of the local situation.

Having your entire Election Day operation work out of the
main campaign headquarters reduces the chances of duplication and increases the possibilities of tight, centralized control. Legal help can be made readily available, as can baby-
sitting facilities and transportation pools for voters. On the
other hand, the situation is often hectic, and enough tele-
phones are usually not available for all the precinct captains
to make their phone calls to people who have not yet voted.

In rural areas like the 2nd Congressional District of California, which stretches 500 miles from the Oregon border
down into Southern California, decentralization is essential.
In such a district, several headquarters must be set up. Decentralization is sometimes a good idea in city districts as
well. A decentralized operation increases familiarity with local
conditions and neighborhood peculiarities, especially in areas
with heavy ethnic concentrations. Someone helping the precinct poll watcher can probably make the phone calls and
arrange rides to the polls just as easily from his home as from
central headquarters, provided that he has been briefed on

just what is expected of him and has a car handy. A decentralized approach also serves to curb somewhat that bane of all organizations—creeping bureaucratization. The fewer the people around campaign headquarters during Election Day, the better the probability that workers with truly functional, assigned tasks will be able to carry them out.

In any type of decentralized operation, of course, it is essential that someone at the central headquarters be assigned the primary task of liaison and co-ordination with the local units and be ready to supply them with services, such as legal aid, that could not be effectively produced at the local level.

In the week before Election Day, contact all your "sure" voters (those you have rated 1) to remind them to vote and to find out if you can do anything (e.g., provide baby sitters or car rides to the polling places) to make it easier for them to get to the polls. This is why the precinct leader must keep an up-to-date, inclusive hard card file. Such a file eases considerably his task of selecting every voter in the precinct with a good probability of voting for his candidate. On the Sunday evening before the election, all precinct leaders should gather at the campaign headquarters to estimate the vote in their precincts and to present a general political intelligence report on their precinct to the campaign manager. All these efforts result in effective voter mobilization on Election Day.

Election Day is the culmination of all the hard work and effort of the preceding months. So that these efforts will pay off, set up a well-organized schedule for election day. Make sure that baby-sitting services and transportation are ready.

See that every precinct is manned by poll watchers and challengers who have been carefully instructed in local election laws and the valid reasons for challenging voters. It is relatively simple to prevent an unqualified person from voting and nearly impossible to invalidate his ballot once it has been cast.

Fraud, although uncommon, is not unheard-of. It is likely to be a problem primarily in areas of overwhelming one-party domination where election board judges and workers of both parties are hard to find. To ensure the integrity of the polls where machines are used:

1. Be at the polling place when the machines are opened to make sure all the numbers are set at zero.
2. If a machine becomes jammed, call the election board immediately and be sure to get names, addresses, and telephone numbers from the voters then in the polling place.
3. Keep your own tally of the number of people who cast votes.
4. Have a poll watcher present at all times to prevent opposition voters from running up the total by casting multiple votes.
5. Pay careful attention when the numbers are transcribed from the machine to the tally sheet.

Fraud is much more likely to occur when paper ballots are used and during the counting. Be there before the polls close for the count, and stay until the tally sheets are turned in. Watch for attempts to spoil ballots, to illegally invalidate them, or simply to throw them away. One of Senator Birch Bayh's campaign managers in Indiana tells how a flashlight saved the senator fifty votes in a rural district. An overzealous opposition election judge was simply slipping the ballots he didn't like out an open window. Aided by a flashlight, the Bayh forces were able to retrieve the lost ballots from a nearby cornfield. Fraud is seldom so blatant, and it is probably less prevalent than many people believe. It can be eliminated almost entirely by alert and knowledgeable Election Day work.

The presence of a poll watcher is in itself a major deterrent to fraud. The Election Day worker need devote little time to legal and technical problems. His major task is to bring his candidate's supporters to the polls. Each precinct leader compiles a list, in triplicate, of all voters who, on the basis of canvassing information, appear to support his candidate. Each poll watcher receives the list for his election districts and checks off the voters as they come to vote. At intervals of four, two, and one hour before the polls close, a runner collects the lists and takes them to campaign headquarters, where a telephone crew calls voters whose names haven't been checked off, reminds them to vote, and asks if they need assistance in getting to the polls.

Challenging and pulling (getting voters to the polls) have top priority on Election Day, but if manpower is plentiful, last-minute electioneering may have an impact on voters who are still undecided. State laws closely limit the activities permitted in the vicinity of the polls. Electioneering is usually prohibited within a hundred feet of the entrance to the polling place. Outside these limits, most voters can be handed a last-minute propaganda message to read on their way in. This is often a palm card showing the candidate's name on the ballot and a short, pointed message recalling the major themes and motifs of previously distributed brochures. Handouts at factory gates (if factory workers can be counted upon for your candidate) and at commuter and subway stations reminding people that the polls are still open, sound trucks in the districts which canvassing has shown to be most firmly committed to your side, and similar last-minute devices may also prove very worthwhile in an off-year, low-interest election. By noon on Election Day only a very small proportion of the vote usually have been cast yet many candidates have essentially ended their campaign the day before. We strongly suggest that media efforts—particularly on radio and in morning newspapers—be continued (if it is legal) at least until midday on the day of decision.

Useful as these last-minute reminders may prove, they

should not siphon off manpower from getting out the vote operations which can be expected to bring anywhere from two to ten forgetful supporters to the voting booth per election worker. Few media appeals, sound trucks, or leaflets can offer that kind of pay-off.

If an effective, well-organized program has been employed and your candidate did not start the race hopelessly behind, election night can be a gratifying experience. Downcast faces, dark mutterings about "ballot stuffing" and "stealing votes" can be replaced by smiling workers congratulating each other on carrying out an efficient campaign that led to a tremendous victory.

NOTES

1. Among the first were Paul F. Lazarsfeld, Bernard R. Berelson, and Hazel Gaudet, *The People's Choice* (New York: Duell, Sloan, & Pearce, 1944) and Berelson, Lazarsfeld, and William N. McPhee, *Voting* (Chicago: University of Chicago Press, 1954). The largest and most significant body of research has been carried out by the Survey Research Center of the University of Michigan. Among their publications are Angus Campbell, Gerald Gurin, and Warren E. Miller, *The Voter Decides* (Evanston: Row, Peterson, 1954); Angus Campbell, et al., *The American Voter* (New York, Wiley, 1960) and *Elections and the Political Order* (New York; Wiley, 1966); and numerous articles in social science journals.

2. Campbell, et al., *The American Voter*, p. 121.

3. Kenneth Prewitt and Norman Nie, "Review Article: Election Studies of the Survey Research Center," *British Journal of Political Science*, 1 (October 1971), p. 486.

4. Peter B. Natchez, "Images of Voting: The Social Psychologists," *Public Policy*, 18 (Summer 1970), p. 577.

5. See Walter Dean Burnham, *Critical Elections and the Mainsprings of American Politics* (New York: Norton, 1971).

6. Richard A. Brody, et al., "Vietnam, The Urban Crisis, and the 1968 Presidential Election," *American Political Science Review* (forthcoming).

7. Obviously, this should only be done if the voter is in agreement with or undecided about the position of your candidate on the issue.

8. Abraham Lincoln, *Illinois State Register*, February 21, 1840.

9. Gerald Kramer, "The Effects of Precinct-level Canvassing on Voter Behavior," *Public Opinion Quarterly*, 34 (Winter 1970–71), pp. 560–72.

10. Donald E. Stokes and Warren E. Miller, "Party Government and the Saliency of Congress," in Campbell, et al., *Elections and the Political Order*, pp. 194–211.

CHAPTER 7

THE ECONOMICS AND PLANNING
OF POLITICAL CAMPAIGNS

One of the most depressing sights in politics is the headquarters of a defeated candidate on the day after the election. The posters and decorations that looked so impressive
the day before are suddenly tacky and poorly placed. The
used fliers and brochures have lost their zip. Boxes of buttons and bumper stickers have become worthless junk.

Every candidate and every campaign manager should be
forced to pore through this rubble and sort it out with care.
More vividly than anything we can say here, it would tell
how much wasted effort and sheer nonsense go into every
campaign. Look at this stack of mimeographed sheets—
seven pages on the history of American involvement in Cambodia—did anybody read it? What about these 8-by-10 glossy
photographs of our peerless leader that cost 34 cents each—
what end did they serve? And—oh, my God, look at this—
3,000 paper coffee cups printed with the candidate's name:
How we could have used the media time that money spent
on these cups would have bought!

Gimmicks can be useful in a campaign. So can research.
Glossy photographs may have a place. But the key work in
any campaign, as it is now in our politics, is *priorities*. Where

best do you spend your money? How do you use your time and available resources? The answers to these questions are not easy to come by. Many of the things done in campaigns are done simply because candidates have always done things that way. This is a difficult habit to overcome. Since there is no exact science of politics and persistence seems to be one logical strategy. It may be that bumper stickers are a waste of money, but who wants to be the first to experiment in finding out that they aren't?

We know a lot more about voter motivations, about techniques of propaganda, about uses of media, and about effective campaign strategies than ever before. A whole profession of professional campaign consultants has come to play an increasingly important political role, especially in national and state campaigns.[1] Most congressional candidates cannot afford such help; and even in campaigns for higher office, the burdens of most day-to-day operations are borne by unpaid volunteers. And they are often performed quite well. The distinction between amateur and professional, it is worth remembering, is simply that one is paid and the other is not. Some amateurs, some volunteers are highly skilled. It is important to seek out and to use such talents. Some professionals, conversely, are not as smart as they are arrogant. Few of them, moreover, may know the lay of the land in your state or district. Given the fact that professional help costs money, it should be sought with care.

Our purpose in this chapter is to sort out some of the major considerations that go into financing political campaigns and determining how the money should be spent. In particular we are concerned with the role of volunteer activists in the over-all financial planning of a campaign: how can they help to raise money and see that it is wisely spent? Under what conditions should volunteer activities be supplemented by professional help? What are some of the ethical and legal constraints that shape the ways in which campaigns can and should be run?

MONEY

Every two years, the staunchest congressional proponents of law and order openly violate state and federal laws on campaign finances. Under the Corrupt Practices Act of 1925, for example, no candidate for the Senate could spend more than $25,000 on his campaign, no candidate for the House more than $5,000. Even without considering the effects of inflation, such limitations were so unrealistic to begin with that it is little wonder they were never enforced. "I daresay," said Representative James C. Wright (D., Texas) before the House Administration Committee in 1966, "there is not a member of Congress, myself included, who has not knowingly evaded [this law] in one way or another."

If there are no effective legal constraints on the amount a candidate can spend, there are no mental ones either. "Losers," as Jeff Fishel puts it, "are almost always convinced that another $5,000 or $25,000 would have reversed the outcome."[2] And there are few winners with the assurance of a Sam Ervin, who, in his 1972 Senate campaign, actually returned almost 20 per cent of the contributions sent him on the grounds they weren't needed.

The Sam Ervins of the world are rare if not unique. When the Grand Clong strikes, finances are usually the cause of the panic. If such fears cannot be eliminated, they can be alleviated in part by effective fund-raising techniques and through careful planning. Few politicians will ever have enough money to spend; fewer still use what resources they have to maximum effect.

FUND RAISING

There are two ways in which volunteers can help relieve the financial woes of a campaign. One is through direct fund-raising efforts. The other is by providing services that would otherwise have to be paid for out of the campaign budget.

There are thousands of ways to raise money. The best way is simply to ask for it. No gimmick is more effective than peer-group contact. If your target is a millionaire, the approach should be made by a fellow millionaire. Students should put the screws on fellow students; professors, on professors. And don't just ask for money—name the amount you want. If a candidate is worth your spending time on his campaign, surely he is worth more than 50 cents or a dollar from someone who shares your views and knows who you are. There is no substitute for the direct approach. Most people would prefer to give $10.00 outright than pay that amount for a rubber-chicken dinner and three hours of speeches.

There is no substitute for big money. Some people, with a flick of the pen, can give more money in a few seconds than 100 volunteers can collect in a week. Small contributions, however, are important for ideological reasons and because they buy commitment as well as goods and services. Every individual who makes a contribution, no matter how small, has bought a share of the campaign. On Election Day the chances are good that campaign donors will back their investments with votes. In the 1950s and early 1960s the Democratic party ran "Dollars for Democrats" drives that were highly effective from both points of view. Whether or not they will prove effective in the 1970s is problematic. Now there are so many groups, from the Heart Association to Jehovah's Witnesses, who have adopted the technique of door-to-door solicitation of small contributions that the average householder has built up elaborate and effective means of defense against all solicitation.

DOOR-TO-DOOR FUND RAISING The question of whether door-to-door campaigns for donations are worthwhile is essentially a question of priorities. Suppose that a single canvasser could contact fifty householders in a day. If he spent his time talking about candidates and issues, that time would mean fifty guaranteed customer exposures per day. If he spent that same time collecting money, could he produce enough to buy the equivalent exposure through the radio or television?

REACHING THE CONTRIBUTOR How do you reach the small contributor? In New York City, Mayor Lindsay's 1969 mayoralty campaign averaged $1,000 a day from card tables set up on busy sidewalks. Selling buttons or passing cans at state fairs or places where people have loose change in their pockets can be productive, too. Direct mailings, particularly those aimed at specific target groups by a member of that group—e.g., a doctor writing to his fellow doctors—should be tried, but largely as a last resort. Those in the profession of direct-mail campaigns consider 3 per cent returns as excellent. Still, every campaign should seriously attempt to set up special groups like "Lawyers for Jones," "Professors for Jones," etc., to channel publicity and raise money on a peer-group level. Even with these special committees, however, face-to-face contacts are best, phone calls second most effective, and mail solicitations come in a distant third.

Some fund-raising techniques can and should be organized outside of the campaign office. Events staged under the nominal sponsorship of the party organization or through the co-operative efforts of several candidates may, for example, draw upon a different pool of potential contributors than those held on behalf of any single candidate. In 1970 a student-faculty group at the University of Rochester used the device of an antiwar petition as a means of raising funds for antiwar advertisements and for the support of peace candidates for the congress. The petition was rather innocuously phrased so as to attract large numbers of signatures. Those signing were asked to contribute 50 cent or more to the cause it embodied. In many cases, it would be unethical to channel funds solicited in this way directly into a campaign. Such petition drives could, moreover, seriously waste valuable manpower. But in the dog days of July and August or before supportable candidates have emerged for the primary, devices similar to the Rochester petition could provide effective devices for recruiting volunteers, for training them in door-to-door work, for compiling lists of sympathetic voters, and for raising the funds necessary to dramatize an issue which might later be crucial to the campaign.

DINNERS, EVENTS, DRINKS, AND CELEBRITIES The time-honored way of raising political money in the United States is through the planned event, be it a cocktail party, a country fair, or formal dinner. The obvious problem with such methods is that overhead costs—both in terms of time and money—can be prohibitive. No one particularly likes to pay $25.00 for $5.00 worth of food and drink, so having a name speaker, or a good band, or first-rate entertainment helps. There are people who will budget themselves $10.00 a year for politics and $25.00 a week for entertainment whose pockets you simply couldn't get into in any other way. So it is important that the event be fun. More importantly, the appeal to attend should, if possible, be personal rather than ideological. Those who are highly committed to a cause will contribute anyway. What you are seeking, in staging special events, are the marginally committed, and the way to get them is through personal contact. Your core group of volunteers, for example, can go through the mailing list and write a personal note on each invitation sent to a personal acquaintance. Or ten or twelve key volunteers can host pre-dinner cocktail parties before a fund-raising event to which they invite friends who, naturally, are expected to attend the dinner.

Celebrities can be a factor in enhancing the appeal of a fund-raising event—as Spiro Agnew illustrated during the off-year campaigns of 1970. But the best names are likely to be booked long in advance, and the lesser lights unknown to your target audience. Sometimes local notables are your best drawing cards.

OUTSIDE GROUPS   It is often a source of surprise to novice politicans how difficult it is to attract party money from outside of the district. Having won the nomination, they expect to be courted by lobbyists and lavishly supported by the party hierarchy. Most experienced candidates would agree with the Midwestern challenger who lamented, "Blessed are those who do not expect very much, for they will not be disappointed."[3] Even well-established incumbents receive the bulk of their contributions from local sources. In 1964 it is estimated that the average amounts disbursed by national party groups were $1,224 for Democrats and $2,851 for Republicans. Non-incumbents averaged somewhat less.[4]

Party funds, and those from many interest groups, moreover, are focused disproportionately upon marginal races. In lopsided districts, Huckshorn and Spencer found in 1962, less than half of the candidates running against incumbents received any money at all from national party sources.[5] We have, perhaps, made the point; but Fishel sums it up well:

> The luckiest Democratic candidate, competing in a tight, marginal district, might have received $5,000 from all national-level party committees. Add to this figure $3,500–$5,000 from nonparty sources (mainly COPE); the result is that only one-sixth to one-tenth of total campaign-related expenses come from national finance sources. Nor are Republicans much better off in this respect. Despite their consistent ability to raise and spend more money, the luckiest GOP challengers were fortunate in receiving . . . more than $10,000, again one-sixth to one-tenth the total cost.[6]

It is foolish then, to count upon outside help. But it is possible to enhance one's chances of getting such help. In 1970, for example, James Abourezk ran as a Democrat in a South Dakota district which previously had been 58 per cent Republican. Normally, a contest such as this would be considered beyond hope; but Abourezk prepared so persuasive a six-page statistical and descriptive analysis of his chances for winning that he was able to attract some outside funds from groups like the National Committee for an Effective Congress and the Universities National Anti-War Fund. These funds, though useful, met but a fraction of total needs. Abourezk's optimism, however, proved justified and his backers were rewarded by a close but significant victory.

MONEY AND THE CAMPAIGN   The campaigns to raise funds to win votes tend to be conducted separately. The finance chairman is the odd-ball of most campaign organizations. In a sense he must be, for the target groups of fund-raisers and vote-getters are significantly different. A case can be made, however, for bringing large numbers of volunteers into the fund-raising part of the campaign. Michael Walzer, for example, suggests that "the best way to get money is to earn it. . . . Fund raising," he argues,

> is an important activity because it enables large numbers of people to express their support for the movement in ways that also utilize their everyday competence and give them something important to do. Among the most demoralizing features of political life are the long spells of inaction. . . . Fund-raising is both time-consuming and useful. Many people are accustomed to it and do it well; and the sense of a job to be done that can be done is a crucial factor in generating loyalty to the cause and self-confidence in the activists.[7]

These arguments apply best, it should go without saying, to campaigns that begin early and have an abundance of volunteers.

SPENDING THE LOOT

Moneygivers, like voters, often decide late. Button makers and printers, however, do not usually like to wait to be paid. Indeed, candidates for public office are such notoriously bad risks, that most commercial enterprises demand cash-on-the-barrelhead and will refuse to deliver until paid in full. Even if money can be raised early in the campaign, the problems of setting rational budgets are among the most difficult, complex, and important of politics. It is embarrassing to be caught short. Few things are scarcer than contributions to the campaigns of those who have already lost. It is worse than embarrassing, however, to end a losing campaign with money in the bank. Because media time must be booked in advance, a campaign that underestimates its October revenues may literally find it hard to know what to do with its money.

What must be underscored, then, is the vital importance of careful budgeting and planning of the cash flow of the campaign. If outside professional help can be afforded, this is an area in which it is often most needed. A good budget, as Hank Parkinson says, is more than a guide to how the campaign will be run. "It's also a sales tool for raising money," particularly among larger contributors who want some assurance that their money will be well spent.[8]

There is a lot of guesswork that goes into the preparation of a campaign budget: how much you spend depends on how much you can get, and that is not always easy to predict. The first step, then, is to try to predict when and how you will get your money: how much from national and party sources, how much from big donors, middle-sized donors, and small contributions; how much from special events, along with a schedule of when they will be held, and so on. The time schedule is particularly important. When this schedule is matched against a comparable list of outlays and the cash flow of the campaign is planned, you will know whether or not loans need to be arranged, what adjustments need to be made in the fund-raising schedule, and so on. More importantly, the cash-flow budget provides a guide during the campaign as to how you are doing.

Most campaigns begin with three budgets: an "oh-no-it's-bad" or minimal set of figures on what it will cost simply to put the show on the road; a realistic appraisal based on what you can most probably expect to raise; and a pie-in-the-sky appraisal of what it would be nice to have to win. The cash-flow budget at any point in the campaign can be used as a check on which of these projections seems most realistic.

The minimal budget for a campaign begins with basic candidate and organizational expenses: travel, printing, supplies, the phone, headquarters, and staff if it must be paid for. Almost all additional funds are for advertising and public relations. Budgeting here is a three-dimensional problem. First, there is a time dimension: thirty seconds on TV in the week before the election is a good deal more important than thirty seconds a month earlier. These problems of timing, however, must be closely related to the second dimension the choice of campaign advertising, the selection of appropriate media. Ideally, the "heavier" media, those which reach more intelligent audiences, should be used early in the campaign when the more involved and intelligent voters make up their minds. In the final weeks, when the target group is the least informed and least politically sophisticated voters, low-involvement media such as television receive top priority. This kind of schedule cannot always be maintained. Television time must usually be booked and paid for well in advance, radio is more flexible, and newspapers and brochures are the most flexible of all.

The third dimension of the public relations budget involves the problem of targeting. Which parts of the district are most important? We have covered the problem of targeting for door-to-door activities in earlier chapters; the considerations governing uses of media should be based on the same indexes of priorities. But there are some other considerations. For example, a candidate for the House of Representatives in northern Indiana can practically rule out television: he must pay for the entire Chicago market in order to reach his target group of voters.

Obviously we have only scratched the surface of a very complex set of problems. The more money you have, moreover, the more complex these problems become and the greater the need for expert help. If your total budget for advertising and public relations is, say, less than $20,000, almost all of it should go to buying time and space. You will be lucky simply to get your candidate's name across to the average voter, and it is downright silly to spend $10,000 preparing TV spots which you don't have the money to show them. The bigger the budget, the more prominently such things as polls, professional agencies, and production costs should figure in to it.

Of all areas of campaign strategy, this is one of the most difficult about which to generalize. Money is important, but elections can be won without it. Techniques of fund raising that are effective in one part of the country may prove utter disasters elsewhere.

A major cause of divorce in the United States is argument over money. It is also a major cause of dispute within political campaigns. There are no magic formulas; but there is one rule of absolutely vital import: a campaign without a cash-flow budget, without some concrete plan of economic priorities, is in serious trouble before it starts.

HIRING EXPERTISE

Volunteer efforts can frequently be used to offset a campaign's lack of funds. Because they have a personal touch, which not even television can match, many volunteer activities are highly effective in penetrating the fog of indifference that envelops the average voter. There is no substitute for direct voter contact with a candidate, but a personal visit from one of his workers runs a close second.

Volunteers can also play an important part in putting a campaign together. It is ironic how frequently local talents are underutilized in volunteer campaigns: a professional writer spending her time going door to door while a salesman writes press releases. At the same time, few volunteers are experienced in the peculiar arts of political campaigns. Aspiring politicians cannot, as a rule, learn by experience: a campaign is a one-shot enterprise. Thus for candidates with money and a touch of common sense, professional campaign consultants can be very useful. Polling, finances, and media use are specific areas in which there are real skills that can be purchased. By hiring outside consultants, moreover, a campaign can acquire objectivity as well as experience, and this may be its strongest point.

PHONIES AND PHENOMENA   Campaign management has become a big business. Almost every candidate running for the U. S. Senate in a competitive state, along with quite a few House aspirants, will use outside, professional help in 1974. Many of these candidates will turn to specialists, such as polling agencies or media producers, only for the performance of highly technical and specific assignments. But a large and growing number will hire professional managers to define and establish the basic outlines of their campaigns. Their task, ideally, is to build rational planning, clear strategy, and modern technology into the campaign.

As in all professions, the quality of campaign consultant work varies enormously. It is hard to conceive that Milton Shapp ever could have been elected governor of Pennsylvania without Joseph Napolitan. The contrasts between the media campaigns of most candidates and those with top-flight advisers (e.g., David Garth for John Lindsay, Spencer-Roberts for Ronald Reagan, Charles Guggenheim for the Kennedys) are so striking as to make comment unnecessary.

At the other extreme is the actual experience of a candidate who ran as a Democrat against an entrenched Republican incumbent a few years ago. Enthralled by the brochure of a campaign management firm that boasted never to have lost an election, our man, B, plunked down $100,000 for a complete package of campaign management and organization. The only tangible outgrowths of this expenditure were billboards and small signs bearing the cryptic slogan "Do Better with B." If anybody did better, it was clearly the management firm. B lost very badly and in more ways than one.

Few professional consultants are charlatans. A good one can provide—in a matter of hours—invaluable advice and ideas. Even a low-budget campaign can often actually save money by hiring the expertise of a top-flight consultant early in the game.

One final word of warning is, however, in order. The goal of the campaign consultant is to rationalize the use of information on constituency characteristics and campaign resources. "Too many campaigns try to fly by the seat of their pants," says William Roberts of Spencer-Roberts. "Good old Charley Brown who knows that district like the back of his hand just isn't good enough for this day and age."[9] Good old Charley, however, may be important for other reasons and may take offense at being ignored. Conflict between experienced locals and "outsiders" is almost inevitable and must be handled with care.

THE COMPUTER GAME   As we noted in Chapter 3, one of the things that made the Movement for a New Congress good press copy in 1970 was its use of computers both in evaluating candidates and in placing volunteers. Actually, the work done by the computers was very simple and could have been handled in other ways. But, as Robert Chartrand puts it:

> Automatic data processing can serve as a valuable aid to the campaign workers by organizing, storing, and making available a surprising variety of information. Hundreds of hours of laborious manual handling of registration data can be replaced—with the aid of a carefully devised system—by the processing capabilities of the electronic computer. Lists of workers, voters, funding sources, and special interest groups can be prepared in a variety of formats within a relatively brief time. This can mean that during special registration drives, or on election day, when time is of the essence, the worker can function at peak efficiency.[10]

The computer, however, does not perform miracles. Although a precinct targeting sheet looks more impressive on an IBM printout, it is no different than one prepared by hand. Some of the worst charlatans in the field of campaign consulting do little more than transpose information you already have sorted into a more impressive format. One company in 1972, for example, charged 2 cents per name for, in effect, reprinting telephone directories on IBM paper. Still, the computer can be an invaluable adjunct to a volunteer-based door-to-door campaign, and it is a virtual necessity for effective direct mail. There may be local talent available for effective programming. It may be possible to get computer time donated. If not, the money spent for good computer work is probably well spent. Good politics, as we said earlier, is in large part a matter of good lists. Unless your manpower pool is unlimited, there is no matching the computer's ability to sort and classify such lists.

TO POLL OR NOT TO POLL?

Many people, exposed only to the periodic reports of George Gallup and Louis Harris that appear in the press, think that the most important function of a poll is to find who is ahead at a certain juncture in the race. From a campaign perspective, this is its least important function. The purpose of a sample survey is to locate issue publics, or groups with identifiable interests and concerns, and indicate the best ways of exploiting public attitudes toward the candidate and his platform. The smart politician, as we argued in Chapter 1, hunts where the ducks are. Polls are a means of locating the ducks, and they have three important uses:

> The first of these is the key group breakdowns that dissect the political anatomy of the constituency, indicating area differences, racial and religious patterns, nationality-group differences, occupational patterns (including unions and farm workers), differences by size of place, and how the vote in prior years is now dividing. Such a lay of the land is vital to a candidate, for it enables him to figure out just where he can put together his majority.[11]

The second area of usefulness is in what a poll can tell a candidate about his personal standing with the voters. "Voters," Harris says, "tell polltakers things that not even his best friends would tell him."[12] Objectivity, as we have said before, is hard to come by during a campaign and must sometimes be bought. Polls are useful because they provide "hard" data on what really are the strong and weak points of a candidate's image.

> A third area of useful information [which polls can provide] is the definition of issues. . . .
> The issues thus defined are analyzed not only by key groups but, more importantly, by switchers—people who voted for one party in a previous election and now are switching to the other party in this election. This concept of switching is crucial. . . . For when the electorate is analyzed by the hard-core vote for each candidate and the switchers for each candidate, then we can see which issues are firming up the sound base of a candi-

date, which are bringing voters over to him, and which are losing him votes.[13]

Many professional campaign specialists will not begin their work without a poll. But professional polls are expensive, so expensive that despite their known importance less than one House candidate in ten has ever used them. The decision on whether or not to poll is usually a financial one, and it is true that the candidate who probably most needs to poll is the one whose campaign is primarily media-based.

The personal-contact campaign can benefit enormously from a good poll. It is essential in planning literature, in targeting, and in briefing volunteers to know your constituency. Feedback from canvassers is an important source of such information and should be systematically collected; but the hunches, guesses, and evaluations of activists and volunteers are often the worst possible guides to district opinion. Politeness is easily mistaken for positive attitudes toward the candidate. The particular issues that bring volunteers into a campaign seem, to their ears, to be on every voter's lips. Canvassers, moreover, usually begin to work long after major strategic decisions have been made.

It is not always necessary to hire a professional polling organization in order to get some of the information a poll provides. Aggregate-data analysis can also be used to locate swing voters, identify areas of party strength, and, in some cases, to locate key subgroups in the district. In one sense, aggregate-data analysis is superior to polling. It is based on hard data about what people really did in the voting booth rather than on what they said they did. Its two major shortcomings are, first, what W. S. Robinson has called "the ecological fallacy" and, second, the problem of not being able to fit data on past elections precisely to the needs of the present.

The "ecological fallacy" is that of assuming that the behavior of individuals can reliably be inferred from the behavior of groups. As Backstrom and Agranoff put it in an excellent article on the uses of aggregate data:

> If in a precinct of 150 voters, 100 (67%) voted for Candidate A in one race, and 100 (67%) voted for Candidate X in a second race, we can't be sure that they are the same 100 people. . . . Likewise, if the Republican candidate in a black ghetto precinct gets 10% of the vote, we do not know if 10% of the blacks are voting Republicans; it may be their remaining few white neighbors.[14]

The "ecological fallacy" limits what may be inferred from aggregate-data analysis, but it does not seriously detract from its use in planning and managing important aspects of a campaign. A more serious limitation derives from the nature of the data at hand. Unlike a poll, aggregate data cannot tell us about voter images of the candidates. Last year's data, moreover, may be of limited use today: the Humphrey-Nixon-Wallace breakdown from 1968, for example, was not a very good predictor of how people would vote in 1972 when confronted with Nixon and McGovern. Similarly, the McGovern vote in 1972 is not a very reliable indicator of Democratic party strength in 1974.

Aggregate-data analysis, then, is primarily useful in targeting and in planning the over-all geographic strategy of a campaign. A public opinion survey serves to identify more specific voter attitudes and to determine strategies of image and issue emphasis. In a door-to-door campaign it can help volunteers to be better informed about the electorate with which they are dealing.

HOW TO POLL   Badly done, a poll can be worse than useless. A little knowledge, especially if inaccurate, is a dangerous thing. Most professional polling organizations are reasonably reliable; but before investing the $5,000 to $20,000 usually charged, the wise candidate will check carefully on the qualifications of his pollster. It is possible, with help, to conduct a volunteer-based poll. But some kind of semiprofessional help is essential in devising the questionnaire to be used and drawing the sample to be polled.

Any survey of public opinion must have a well-chosen sample. A poll surveys only a small part of the electorate. The larger the sample, the more costly the poll, whether it is done door to door, by telephone, or through the mails. The sample must accurately reflect the proportion of the various groups in the constituency. A number of factors come into play in selecting the sample: income, race, occupation, area of residence, religion, party affiliation, sex, age, ethnicity, propensity to vote. Any factor that is itself significant in electoral politics must be considered in drawing up a sample. Having a properly weighted sample is so important that professional advice and help must be sought here.

The professional pollster must be told what the campaign needs to know before a questionnaire is drawn up. It may be decided to sample the districts all at once. Or an opinion sample on one specific issue may be conducted within one age, income, or ethnic group. The questions asked in each type of survey will vary accordingly. But the point is simply that you cannot design a useful poll without a clear idea of what it is that you need to know and why.

University students often have access to people who know sampling procedures and can construct questionnaires. Major public opinion survey groups exist, for example, at the University of Chicago and the University of Michigan. Many social scientists do opinion surveys as part of their scholarly work. Many students have also done survey analysis. Some of the volunteers may themselves have expertise here.

But before proceeding with a public opinion survey, volunteers had better be sure that those claiming to be experts do know what they are about. Sometimes persons who work for a professional polling agency will be willing to help out on an individual basis.

USING POLLS   Stephen Schadegg and some other campaign consultants stress the importance of momentum in campaigns, of building toward a peak of strength on Election Day. There is, they argue, a bandwagon effect which influences the less-informed swing-voters to switch to a candidate who appears to be winning or gaining strength. A poll, even if poorly done, which shows your candidate gaining strength may thus be useful as a psychological tool in the campaign. Certainly it can be an important weapon in fund raising, and it can be important in maneuvering for group and party support in the preprimary stage of a campaign. John F. Kennedy, for example, won over a number of skeptical party leaders in 1960 with a poll showing that the Catholic issue would help rather than hurt his chances of carrying the major states. A poll which gives bad news is seldom released to the press.

Most incumbents and many challengers now conduct polls among their constituents on their attitudes toward important issues. These are in no sense scientific surveys, and they are seldom taken as such by those who send them out. Usually the questionnaires are sent to every household or registered voter in the district and the rate of return varies from 5 to 50 per cent. The purpose is not—as it might appear—to find what people think. The bias of the procedures makes pools such as these worthless in that sense. They do convey to the voter, however, a sense of concern; they may locate some interesting issue attitudes that warrant more systematic concern; most important, the returned questionnaires are a goldmine of information in compiling lists.

THE PROBLEM OF CORRUPTION

Devices such as "phony" polls offend some people's sense of fair play. It is cynical if not immoral, they feel, to manipulate the electorate as if it were incompetent, to substitute gimmicks and devices for honest, straight talk about the issues. Outright dishonesty—lying about your candidate or his opponent—has no place in a campaign; it is immoral and it often turns out to be bad politics. But the average voter is probably not interested in the "whole truth" either. Not everyone cares about his congressmen's attitudes toward rural electrification, foreign aid to India, or situs picketing. To convey an honest image, to give the voter just one new bit of information, is dramatically to increase the over-all rationality of the electoral process. Any device that carries your campaign over the threshold of indifference and contributes to the creation of an informed electorate is justifiable.

In politics, as in most aspects of life, one puts one's best foot forward. The touchstone of political decision-making is votes. As Baus and Ross put it with regard to budgeting, the question which always must be asked is, "How many votes will *this* expenditure, *this* program, *this* office, *this* mailing produce?"[15] Political morality may differ in some ways from general morality—politicians have to court voters. But there are limits—legal, practical, and moral that—Watergate to the contrary notwithstanding—apply to virtually all American political campaigns.

THE LAW   Whatever constraints there are on the behavior of American politicians, few of them are written into law. Even the laws of libel and slander tend to be enforced far less strictly with regard to candidates for public office than for others.

Every campaign should, nonetheless, have competent legal advice. In addition to technical requirements for getting on the ballot, deputizing poll-watchers, and the like, new state and federal laws on campaign financing impose rather strict reporting requirements on candidates for public office. Whether or not these requirements will be strictly enforced depends, we suspect, upon the vigilance of volunteer activists in monitoring the opposition. The key provision of the

1973 federal law is the requirement that the names and addresses of all substantial contributors be publicly reported. Such reporting requirements are meaningless, however, unless someone performs the laborious tasks (a) of checking the names to see what hidden interests (if any) they represent, and (b) of confirming that, the total amount reported bears a reasonable resemblance to the amount spent. (You can estimate how much your opponent spends by comparing your own costs against his use of brochures, bumper stickers, media time, billboards, etc.)

It should go without saying that you should be absolutely meticulous in reporting your own finances. And although it is not required by law, we think it desirable—and usually good politics—for every candidate for public office to disclose his own financial interests and to pledge himself to divestiture of all holdings which might produce conflicts of interest.

POLITICAL ETHICS Campaign contributors, even those who donate big money, seldom demand exact *quid pro quos*. What money does usually buy, however, is access to or the right to be heard by an office holder. It is very difficult for a newly elected congressman to refuse to see a person who has just contributed $5,000 to his campaign. Because it is difficult to deny such access, some care should be exercised in screening major contributors. It is not paranoid to be very cautious, however—your candidate may have a hard time explaining if, for example, one of his major backers is later indicted for some crime.

Ideally, campaigns could be run on public funds or from the donations of numerous small contributors. In reality, an adequately financed campaign must depend heavily on a few affluent angels. What are they buying? A congressman from a marginal district, for example, who votes "right" on peace-related issues receives a $3,000 contribution from the Council for a Livable World—is his vote being "bought"? We think not, but the issue can be a troubling one when the contribution in question comes from a controversial group or individual.

In the wake of Watergate, a few rules seem more clear than ever: any contributor who demands anonymity, who wants to contribute through a dummy organization, or who demands a *quid pro quo* for his money should be shown to the door. Rules such as these may seem so obviously correct as to hardly warrant mention; but in the heat of the campaign it is surprising—as the Watergate inquiries reveal—how many principles heretofore honorable men will sacrifice in the service of a "higher cause."

Money is not the root of all political evils. Most of us like to believe that the causes for which we are working are just. Our opponents, by force of logic, are ergo, backing causes that are unjust, if not downright evil. Their villainies must be exposed. This attitude, though understandable, can have dangerous consequences.

At the practical level, the temptation to attack often diverts attention from the critical issues of the campaign and prevents a candidate from fully developing his own themes and image. Attacks on the opposition, moreover, frequently backfire. The old adage "Never get in a squirting match with a skunk" applies to most campaigns.

Finally, we would suggest that personal attacks on the opposition are basically out-of-bounds. Unless they genuinely inhibit his or her capacities to function in office, the sexual appetites, family relations, or personal problems of a candidate have no place in a campaign. If Senator X's clinical history or Congressman X's drinking habits are to be exposed, leave it to the press. One gains neither respect nor admiration by being the first to assassinate character.

LITTLE WATERGATES: THEIRS AND OURS

The Grand Clong makes mountains of molehills, paranoids of plain folks, and schemers of savants. *Their* campaign always seems incredibly well organized compared with the disorganization of *ours*. *They* roll in money while *we* wallow in poverty. *Our* problems are public knowledge, *theirs* shrouded in secrecy.

There is no rational way to explain why high officials in the Committee to Re-elect the President ordered the bugging of the Democratic National Committee. But the paranoia which produced Watergate is not uncommon. It should be resisted if only because everything you need to know about the opposition is a matter of public record.

Rumors will abound. Few are worth worrying about. Almost none demand action. The campaign which in any way becomes seriously involved in reacting to the real or imagined moves of the opposition is in serious trouble.

Ninety-nine times out of a hundred the stock phrase "Nothing much will come of it" applies to crisis situations in a campaign. Ninety-nine out of a hundred major political blunders coincidentally derive from the tendency to over-react to perceived crises. The competition that counts is the competition for votes, and that contest is won or lost in the public arena, not behind closed doors. As Senator McGovern's failure to arouse public interest in the issue of Watergate illustrates, the public is remarkably uninterested in how politicians run their campaigns.

"DIRTY TRICKS"   During the Senate Watergate Hearings, one Republican campaign official encountered Democrat Dick Tuck in the Capitol hallway: "You started this, Tuck," he said. In a sense he was right. Tuck's speciality was bizarre campaign tricks, and he took special delight in bedeviling Richard Nixon. During the 1962 gubernatorial contest in California, for example, Democrat incumbent Pat Brown attempted to make an issue of an unexplained loan which the Nixon family had received from the millionnaire recluse Howard Hughes; Tuck managed to persuade the caterer of a Nixon dinner in Chinatown to stuff the fortune cookies with papers asking, "What About the Hughes Loan?" Such tricks are sometimes amusing, but can hardly be recommended. Although they may prove annoying to the opposition, they seldom win votes, often create enemies of potential supporters, and, worst of all, are a waste of valuable time and resources.

Whatever the ethics of Tuck's pranks, the Watergate bugging of the DNC was of a different order. As one senior Republican congressman recently put it to a retired former colleague:

> We have all done things that we aren't proud of. But this stuff is different. I don't think there is a member of this body who ever went so far. This is beyond the pale.

Every candidate should subscribe to and adhere to the Code of the National Fair Campaign Practices Committee. If your opponent violates the code, the violation should be reported immediately. But it is important to avoid the trap of being put on the defensive. One of Lyndon Johnson's favorite stories concerned the rural politician whose campaign manager suggested spreading a rumor that the opposition candidate enjoyed sexual relations with his pigs. "But it isn't true," the candidate protested. "I know," said the campaign manager, "but I'd like to see him try to deny it." Most opposition charges are best ignored: the more outrageous the charge, the more difficult it is credibly to deny.

Ethical politics, we are suggesting, is by and large good politics. Run your own campaign, worry about your own problems, project your own image and issues, and the opposition will take care of itself.

NOTES

1. For an early, but still cogent, analysis of the role of such experts in campaigns, see Stanley Kelley, Jr., *Profes-*

sional Public Relations and Political Power (Baltimore: Johns Hopkins Unversity Press, 1956).

2. Jeff Fishel, *Party and Opposition* (New York: McKay 1973), p. 98.

3. Quoted in Fishel, op. cit., p. 99.

4. Ibid., p. 101.

5. Robert Huckshorn and Robert Spencer, *The Politics of Defeat* (Amherst: University of Massachusetts Press, 1971, p. 151.

6. Fishel, op. cit., pp. 103–4.

7. Michael Walzer, *Political Action: A Practical Guide to Movement Politics* (Chicago: Quadrangle Books, 1971), p. 61.

8. Hank Parkinson, *Winning Your Campaign: A Nuts-and-Bolts Guide to Political Victory* (Englewood Cliffs, N.J.: Prentice-Hall, 1970), p. 63.

9. Quoted in *Congressional Quarterly,* "Campaign Management Grows Into National Industry," *C.Q. Weekly Report* (April 5, 1968), XXVI, p. 707.

10. Robert L. Chartrand, "Information Technology and the Political Campaigner," in Robert Agranoff, *The New Style in Election Campaigns* (Boston: Holbrook Press, 1972), pp. 147–48.

11. Louis Harris, "Polls and Politics in the United States," *Public Opinion Quarterly,* XXVII (Spring 1963), p. 5.

12. Ibid.

13. Ibid., pp. 8–9.

14. Charles H. Backstrom and Robert Agranoff, "Aggregate Election Data in the Campaign: Limitations, Pitfalls, and Uses," in Agranoff, op. cit., p. 165.

15. Herbert M. Baus and William B. Ross, *Politics Battle Plan* (New York: Macmillan, 1968), p. 108.

CHAPTER 8

PROPAGANDA, INTELLIGENCE,
AND RESEARCH

The term "New Politics" has two diverse meanings. On the one hand it refers to a politics founded on new electoral alignments, based on new sets of issues, and cutting across old constituency coalitions.[1] The "New Politics," on the other hand, also refers to new technologies—television in particular —and to the ways in which they have been employed to alter the techniques of campaigning and the content of campaign issues.[2] We have deliberately slighted the second of these interpretations and, in the process, perhaps underestimated the role of the mass media in modern campaigns.

It is possible successfully to run for office entirely through media appeals. Campaigns of the future, it is sometimes argued, will be run entirely by trained specialists in survey and market research and the media arts. The candidate

> will be out front, moving from state to state with robot-like precision, being fed the data from the polls and the simulator. He will no doubt be articulate, and probably he will be handsome and vigorous. And he may or may not be qualified to be President of the United States.[3]

No one could now contemplate a serious race for the presidency or for state-wide office in a major state without heavy reliance on these new technologies. But no one has yet convinced us that without very large amounts of money there is any substitute for face-to-face contact with the voters. Nor is it clear that even a well-financed campaign can project through television alone a strong enough image in and of itself to win an election. The Kennedys were masters at combining volunteer activism and old-time ward politics with high-powered (and high-priced) media blitzes. John Lindsay, conversely, could have bought more votes at $5.00 a head than he won with his television-based 1972 primary campaigns for the Democratic presidential nomination.

The mass media, in short, are important, but local legwork is also. When the two forces are effectively combined they complement each other well. It would be ridiculous, when funds are available, for volunteer activists to eschew the use of media, so long as both means of communication are kept in harmony.

THE SELLING OF THE CANDIDATE

In presidential elections, television has clearly become the single most important campaign media. In polls conducted by the Survey Research Center at the University of Michigan, the percentage of those listing TV as their major source of campaign information rose to 61 per cent in 1960 from 32 per cent in 1952. In that same eight year period, the costs of running for office in the United States nearly doubled, and almost all of the extra dollars were used for TV. Richard Nixon in 1972 spent more money on television than both major parties had spent for all campaign costs combined in 1952. Not only has television become the nation's major source of campaign information, it has also become the most credible. For more than a decade, surveys have ranked television as more believable a source of news to most

Americans than any other medium. It has, moreover, the advantage of being a "low-effort" medium. Unlike a newspaper ad which must be read, TV demands nothing of its audience but time.

These four critical characteristics of television—widespread acceptance, credibility, cost, and ease of acceptance—have stimulated both exaggerated fears and hopes. On the one hand, it is argued, television has brought politics back to the people—by bringing candidates right into the living rooms of the masses, it has enabled the public to free itself from the influence of various power brokers and influence peddlers, and directly to judge and evaluate the alternatives presented. It is, this argument goes, an honest medium, one that pitilessly reveals personality and ability: no matter how carefully contrived the appeal, the true nature of the candidate invariably emerges. Books like Joe McGinnis's *Selling of the President,* on the other hand, convey quite different impressions. Here the distorting effects of TV spot promotion are emphasized: its ability to screen out—through careful editing—flaws of character, image, or message; its tendency to oversimplify complex problems; and above all its tendency to substitute image for substance.

Whether or not television can be blamed or praised for tendencies such as these is problematic. Campaigns have always oversimplified complex issues, that, indeed, is one of their chief functions. Since before the time of "Tippecanoe and Tyler Too," when a rather lackluster old man was recalled as the rough-and-tumble Indian fighter he had perhaps been in his prime, personal images have often overshadowed hard issues. There is considerable evidence, however, that the public is far less susceptible to media appeals than either the critics or defenders of TV are willing to allow. "The voter," as Pool puts it,

is not a passive target of the messages of mass media. Rather he is a repository of countless bits of previous information. He retains within him a lifetime of earlier messages that have been structured into a series of pre-dispositions. The new message adds one more, but its net effect in changing the balance is infinitesimal compared to its effect as a trigger to responses already determined by predispositions. At any one moment the voter's predisposition is likely to be a far better predictor of his response to a stimulus than the character of the stimulus.[4]

Through constant exposure to biased appeals the average American has become relatively adept at filtering and evaluating propaganda. Because of their brevity, political campaigns in particular tend to stand out as things to be guarded against. "Up go the voters' defenses against being 'propagandized'—especially by the opposition political party. The result is often tune-out rather than turnout."[5] Even at the well-financed presidential level,

Political campaigns seem to be peculiarly impotent in moving the masses of voters away from their original choices. A small proportion of voters who are interested in politics make use of any source of information to satisfy their desire for additional knowledge, but these voters seek to educate themselves mostly about their own choices of candidates. . . . The unmotivated remain relatively politically naive, and all the pleadings of press, radio, and television appear to fail in their missions of direct persuasion-conversion.[6]

Two effects of television do seem clear. First, it has made running for major office far more expensive. "Money and politics," as one recent study notes, "have always been inextricably interrelated, but the restrictive cost of television campaigning threatens to make politics even more of a rich man's game."[7] Second, the public's increasing reliance upon and faith in the credibility of television may have fatefully altered the kinds of messages which the electorate expects to receive during a campaign. Whether or not a candidate can afford to use television, he must project his message to

an audience that has become increasingly video-oriented in
its approach to politics. If nothing else, "It has greatly
extended the purely visual dimension of political communication."[8] Dan Nimmo argues further that the techniques of
television "are usually based on an appeal to the tastes, rather
than the convictions, of Americans, for television advisers
are convinced that personalities and not issue stands or
political parties win votes."[9] Whether or not the importance
of personality has grown, what clearly is different in our
electronic age is the public's expectation of a personally
oriented message. It is not enough to know how a candidate
stands on school busing, we want to see how he deals with
a confrontation on the issue, how he reacts under stress, how
well he can handle a difficult problem.

In the 1st Congress, a member of the House represented
less than 30,000 people. Today the figure is close to half a
million. No candidate obviously can directly contact all
voters: he must rely upon various media—word-of-mouth,
printed, and electronic—to communicate. What television has
done is to create the illusion of personal contact. Thus when
John Kennedy was assassinated, many people felt they had
lost a personal friend, his mastery of the media had been
so effective. This is not the place for a lengthy analysis of the
problems of mass society or the nature of alienated man, but
the public's response to television suggests that there is a
strong craving for visual and personal identity with candidates for public office. To ask whether people vote on the
basis of images or issues may thus be to miss the point, for
the answer really is both. George McGovern, for example,
by changing his stand on the welfare issue and vacillating in
his support of Senator Thomas Eagleton as his running mate
damaged both his image and his substantive standing. Similarly, Barry Goldwater in 1964 made statements which
excited opposition on issue-based grounds and simultaneously
shrouded him in an image of irresponsibility.

What we are suggesting is that the selling of a candidate

involves both image development and issue building. And
the two are fundamentally inseparable. A successful campaign
is one that can develop an over-all theme which unites, in as
simple a form as possible, an honest projection of both the
candidate's personal strengths and his orientations toward
the issues. John Kennedy's "Let's get moving again," combined with his repeated calls for "vigor" in the conduct of
national affairs, conveyed simultaneous images of both the
candidate and his program which were both honest and
effective. Hubert Humphrey's failure in 1968, conversely,
to develop a consistent theme left both his image and his
program fuzzy in the public mind and cost him badly on
Election Day.

WHICH MEDIA? Given unlimited resources, television is
clearly number one. As Joseph Napolitan, one of the strongest
professional advocates of a heavy reliance on TV, notes,
however, a poorly made commercial can be worse than none
at all. "Effective use of television," Napolitan says,

> is the key. Everyone uses television now, but some can-
> didates have yet to realize you can *lose* votes on tele-
> vision. You lose them when you put your guy in front of
> a camera, the kind, you know, where he starts out, "Good
> evening, ladies and gentlemen, my name is Joe Blow and
> I want to talk to you tonight about taxes." When you do
> that you can hear the click of sets being switched or
> turned off all over the state. That sort of program is just
> radio with a light to read by.[10]

Napolitan has been known to spend as much as a third of a
campaign's total media budget on production. When you
deal in TV you are entering one of the most highly competitive media markets there is. Many of the best writers,
artists, actors, and film makers in the world are employed
by Madison Avenue, and as much as $150,000 may go into
the production of a single one-minute spot commercial. When

a cheaply made political message follows the Alka-Seltzer ad it looks, well, cheap.

The first consideration, then, in choosing a media mix is money. Second in importance is the nature of the campaign being waged. Television remains a mass media. Its audience cuts across all economic, political, ethnic, and social boundaries. Its message, therefore, cannot be specialized, must be general in its appeal, and, in the final analysis, bland. At the other pole, direct mail can be precisely targeted and sharply keyed to specific-issue constituencies, but is not particularly effective in reaching those whose political interests are low. Newspaper ads, because they are likely to be read only by the most highly involved and politically articulate, are best used early in the campaign when aiming at opinion leaders in the community. The primary function of bumper stickers, billboards, and posters is to build name recognition; when properly designed, they can also reinforce major themes; and when carefully timed, they can help create the illusion of a bandwagon effect of growing support. Radio, like television, is a relatively low-involvement, low-effort media. It has the advantages of being cheaper than TV and somewhat more selective in its audience appeals: the all-news station, for example, reaches a very different audience than one which offers a steady diet of hard rock. The Republican National Committee, in recent years, has placed a particularly heavy emphasis on radio: if he had the campaign to do over again, John Mitchell said in 1968, his only change would be to use more radio. Particularly in suburban areas, where the average commuter spends upward of ninety minutes a day in his car, radio "reaches an audience largely missed by either newspapers or television."[11]

It is almost impossible to generalize about which media are most effective. In large urban areas, for example, television, radio, and newspapers are not economically viable for legislative candidates; the opposite may hold true in rural areas. The problems of incumbents are very different from those of challengers, who must devote considerably more effort to simple name recognition. Some candidates come across very badly on radio and television, others would be foolish to spend their money in any other way.

An example from Swedish politics illustrates nicely the kinds of considerations that should go into determining an optimal media strategy. In 1956 the Swedish Parliament called for a public referendum on a highly divisive Social Democratic party pension proposal. What makes the campaign interesting from our point of view is that each of the three sides in the controversy was given an equal grant of public funds to finance its campaign for its position. According to a report of this election:

> This placed before the managers of the party machineries very difficult problems of strategy: they knew they had so much money to spend on the campaign but they had very little evidence to guide them in deciding how to use the funds. They all wanted to maximize the returns for each *krona* spent on the campaign but how could they know whether the one strategy would pay off better than another?[12]

The Social Democrats, who led Sweden's largest party, had much at stake in the referendum. Polls had shown that the party was in trouble: few rank-and-file Social Democrats knew that their party was behind the pension plan and many had been swayed by opposition arguments. The party leaders turned to a group of social scientists for advice on how best to use their campaign resources. The answer was straightforward:

> public rallies, posters, leaflets, advertisements . . . would make little impact unless backed by a massive effort to contact, to inform and to stimulate the trusted party workers in each locality, the spokesmen and the active officers of each union, the more articulate members of the

secondary associations tied in with the labor movement and the unions.[13]

As the report notes, it is impossible to say whether or not this strategy was responsible for the Social Democrat's strong showing in the referendum.

But in any situation where the alternatives are novel and unfamiliar it will be essential to reactivate and direct the latent political identifications of the rank-and-file and to bring this about, pressures through the immediate personal environment seem most likely to be effective.[14]

In this sense, the Swedish case illustrates what sudents of personal influence call "the two-step flow of communications," a process in which certain opinion leaders, or "gatekeepers," serve to filter the flow of mass communications between the candidate and the masses.[15] Most of the research that emphasized the importance of this particular two-step flow was conducted in the pretelevision days of the 1940s, and there is some evidence today suggesting that by using TV the candidate is capable of by-passing the other gatekeepers and directly influencing large numbers of people. This is particularly true of presidential campaigns where most people at least have some direct personal knowledge of the candidates and issues at hand. But as the 1967 Roper report on the mass media concluded, "the further a candidate was removed from 'here in town,' the stronger television was as the source of a person's political information."[16] Put the other way, the further one moves from the level of national elections, the more important other sources of information become.

Although there is little empirical data bearing directly on the question, it seems that television is likely to have its greatest impact on those voters whose interest in the campaign is marginal. Such voters lack strong commitments to parties; they tend to decide late and to be highly impervious to political messages, that is, they neither read about politics in the press nor discuss it with their peers. Their decisions are affected by television, in short, because most if not all of their information comes from television. There is no two-step flow to them because there are no politically potent communications channels. Whether or not volunteer activists can serve as surrogate gatekeepers is problematic; we suspect that they can. Voting in a sense is a simple act of choice in which the voter adds up the good things he knows about each candidate, subtracts the bad, and votes for the one with the highest score.[17] For those marginally interested in politics, any information, even so simple a fact as party identification, may be sufficient to determine choice. The volunteer, if he gets past the door, can either reinforce or counteract a video message, but even more importantly he can tune the voter in to politics. This means both the turnout effects we discussed in Chapter 3— getting people to act on the basis of their media-related choices—and what we might call tune-in effects—getting people to be aware enough that there is a campaign going on that they will begin to heed the media messages which normally they might ignore.

This last point is particularly important. Americans have become remarkably adept at ignoring or screening out television ads. How does the advertiser get through? One method involves a combination of repetition and association, the frequent association of a brand name with some real or symbolic representation of the product to be bought. The more the name "Bayer" is linked with the word aspirin, the more likely consumers are to choose Bayer when they buy aspirin: the person who feels he has a super headache, the advertisers hope, will think of it as an Excedrin headache as he steps to the counter to make his purchase. Or a very clever or catchy message—"I can't believe I ate the whole thing"—can be used to the same end. The third approach is to work on the gatekeeper, in this case the druggist, to filter media messages and suggest certain products to the consumer.

The relative effectiveness of these three approaches depends to a large degree on the kind of product being sold. High-fashion ads, for example, seldom appear in the electronic media. Working on the assumption that the opinion leaders in the high-fashion area are generally at least middle-income, clothing manufacturers seldom use TV or popular magazines. Rather their advertising is heavily concentrated in such relatively sophisticated publications as *Esquire, The New Yorker,* and *Vogue.* The evidence from a Katz-Lazarsfeld study suggests that politics is more like headaches than like high fashion, that is, if there is a two-step flow it does not usually travel down class lines from the most wealthy to the least. Thus the maid who takes her fashion cues from her ritzy employer feels quite free to ignore her political opinions and admonitions.

The candidate for public office can seldom rely entirely on just one of the direct approaches, but few candidates for public office have the resources to use both. Or, indeed, to repeat their messages often enough to emulate the first of the approaches discussed above. Even with towers of dollars to spend, they simply do not have the time to build the kinds of associations that have made Bayer number one in aspirin.

The "cleverness" approach is controversial even on Madison Avenue. Sure, some media men will insist, "Try it, you'll like it" became a household cliché, but that doesn't mean that more people bought Alka-Seltzer. The problem is more acute in politics where even the clever message needs reinforcement in order to be turned into action. Headaches bring people into drugstores in the first place, but what brings them to the polls? Here, we would suggest, the role of personal influence remains vital, especially in non-national campaigns.

Television, to summarize, has had an enormous impact on the American political process. In presidential campaigns and in state-wide campaigns for governor and senator, it has enabled well-financed and well-managed candidates to by-pass the two-step flow and communicate directly with average voters. Even here, however, its appeal is largely to those who are most marginal in their commitment to politics and whose inclination to act on the basis of their attitudes is most problematic. To achieve maximum effectiveness then, its messages must be reinforced through other media: people must be tuned in to receive the message and turned out on Election Day.

MASS MEDIA AND VOLUNTEERS. Anyone who has ever run for public office understands intuitively the reality if not the theory of the two-step flow. Many candidates spend more time satisfying their supporters than they do courting the voters. Indeed, one reason that some candidates prefer poll- and media-oriented campaigns is that they free the candidate from the necessity of courting and recourting his most ardent supporters. George McGovern in 1972 continued to raise the question of Vietnam long after general public interest in it had subsided, but this seemed necessary, given the campaign's reliance on volunteer activists who were motivated in large part by the war issue.

Volunteers and other gatekeepers who work informally on behalf of a candidate are by definition more politically aware and involved than the average voter. They decide earlier in the campaign who they are for, they know more about the issues and are more interested in them, and they tend to be more partisan. The appropriate media for recruiting them for a campaign are those which deal specifically and in detail with the issues: direct mail, newspapers, and brochures in particular. This material should be issued very early in the campaign and selectively distributed. To sustain the enthusiasm and interest of volunteers, such devices as personal meetings with the candidate, personal notes of thanks, and so on, can be very important. Many candidates also give them special notebooks or packets of statements on a wide variety of issues for them to use in talking with others.

The more a campaign relies on volunteers, the more important such communications become. It is easy but foolhardy to assume that those who work in the campaign know what is going on. They must be told what is happening and why (and of course it is important for the candidate and his top aides to get as much feedback as possible from those who are in direct contact with the voters). Most importantly, the timing of volunteer activities should be co-ordinated in such a way as to be mutually reinforcing. Before a town is canvassed, for example, it should be hit with a media barrage; after the canvass, a literature drop will reach voters who then probably know what the brochure is all about.

FREE EXPOSURE. The most effective media exposures cannot be bought. Walter DeVries, whose brilliant career as a campaign consultant began with his work for George Romney in Michigan, conducted a postelection survey in 1970 on the relative importance of factors that influenced the voting decisions of marginal and undecided voters. Nine of the ten variables which proved "very important" were "not able to be controlled by the campaign," that is, they could not be purchased or directed by the campaign organization. No advertisements, in any media, ranked in the "very important" group. Television ads, in fact, ranked twenty-fourth. The most important variables were such things as television news and talk shows, face-to-face talks with families, newspaper editorials and stories, and radio news programs.[18]

How does a candidate go about gaining such exposure? Part of it is simply a question of technical skill. The better prepared a press release, the less it has to be edited and revised to fit the media's needs and the more likely it is to be used. Preprepared cassettes, for example, will almost always be aired—if they are short and newsworthy—by local radio stations. Care and time should also be spent in courting reporters, editors, and other important media people. The most important method of getting media attention, however, is to provide good copy, to be newsworthy. This is far more easily said than done. As a general rule, for example, Sunday is a slow news day, so press releases issued then will almost always get good coverage in Monday's papers; but one never knows when a juicy murder, plane crash, or revolutionary coup will push everything to the back pages. Thursday's papers, since they are often heavy in ads, are usually heavy in news as well; but the problem here is that your release is likely to be buried somewhere between the sale at Zeke's and a recipe for fondue.

The only "controllable" item which DeVries' survey found to be "very important" in the minds of the voters was direct contact with the candidate. One of the key roles of volunteers, then, is to bring out the crowds. It is far better for the candidate to go to the voter than to bring the voter to the candidate. Watch the papers for sales, fairs, and special events, and be there. One of the interesting things about personal contacts is that they tend to have a rippling-out effect—more people will say that they met a candidate in their neighborhood than actually did. People will tell their neighbors about a candidate who stops at their door. Walking tours or going from house to house can be very effective even if the candidate only visits every fifth house on the street. Such personal visits to a community, moreover, are news for the local press and should be played up as such.

THE CONTENT OF MEDIA APPEALS. Experiments in mass communications lead to a number of interesting but often contradictory conclusions on the most effective types of appeals. "Scare" messages, for example, are less immediately effective than those founded in reason; but after a few weeks have elapsed, the differences tend to disappear. The one fact which is clear, however, in virtually every study of opinion change is that the audience is the most important variable. Every voter has in his mind certain important reference scales against which he judges candidates, issues, and messages.

The key to a successful propaganda appeal is finding the "weakest link" in the attitude structures of the voter. In 1970, for example, there was substantial latent opposition to the war in Vietnam based on economic considerations. A peace candidate who keyed his opposition to these economic concerns could get his message through to large numbers of voters. One who stressed the "morality" of the war, conversely, would turn most voters off.

One should, above all, lead from strength. If your party has a registration advantage, party loyalty should be emphasized. Canvassing, as we have seen, is more useful in mobilizing latent support than in converting hard-core opponents. It also seems to be true that attitudes are most easily reinforced than changed. People can best be pushed, in other words, in the direction to which they already incline. Thus it cannot be stressed too often that the success or failure of a media campaign depends first and foremost upon a sound knowledge of the audience to which it is directed. As DeVries puts it,

> The ideal (perfect) way to campaign (or govern) is to have a near flawless, up-to-date, two-way communications system between the candidates and the voters and the capability to respond to the information inputs in the system.[19]

POLITICAL INTELLIGENCE

What this means is that in politics as in selling, the admonition in *The Music Man* is crucial: "You gotta know the territory." Polls, we argued in Chapter 7, or aggregate data analysis of a district, are vital adjuncts of the new politics (whichever way that term is defined). "Knowing the territory" means knowing it in terms of the average voter, not as it appears to be to the political pro or dedicated activist.

Information is abundant. Intelligence, that is, well-processed information, is not. The biggest problem here is parochialism, the tendency to assume that the campaign itself is the sun around which all planets revolve. The Copernicus of any campaign is the one who focuses attention back on the voter.

Your Candidate and Theirs

During a heated, pressure-filled campaign it is not hard to see why it is difficult for a candidate to maintain an objective perspective. Self-deception is so common that special steps should be taken to guard against it. The best time for realistic self-appraisal precedes even the decision whether or not to run. Few supporters will have much influence on this decision. Nevertheless, we feel that the question of candidate self-appraisal is such an important one that it should be included in this book even though the book is primarily directed at campaign workers not candidates.

A realistic self-evaluation can help to structure many of the subsequent activities and emphases of the campaign. It should be brutally, ruthlessly honest. Too often a candidate will kid himself into believing that some skeleton is safely interred in his closet, only to be horrified when, for example, his opponent gleefully discloses during the last week of the campaign that he was once caught cheating on a college exam.

Very early on the candidate should go off by himself and honestly answer the following questions[20]:

1. What are your three greatest personal assets as a candidate? (These could be public speaking ability,

public image, extensiveness of contacts, looks, personality.)

2. What are your three greatest personal weaknesses? (Here's where the honesty comes in. Although it may hurt to admit to some of these weaknesses, it will pay off later on.)

3. What things in your background will be campaign assets? (He may be a long time resident of the area or former all-state basketball player).

4. What things in your background will be campaign liabilities? (A messy divorce or affair that is generally unknown; some business deals that while technically legal could be portrayed as being on the shady side.)

5. Beyond what you can personally control, what factors are assets? (Being black in a predominantly black area; having enough money to take care of campaign funding if need be.)

6. Beyond what can be personally controlled, what factors are liabilities? (Being a Catholic in a predominantly WASP or Jewish area; being a woman who has a husband who wishes she stayed in the kitchen instead of being out on the hustings.)

7. Who are five people who can definitely be counted on to work for you throughout the campaign? (You will need people to man five principal positions: campaign manager, fund-raising chairman, volunteer chairman, activities chairman—coffees, walking tours, speaking dates, etc.—and public relations chairman. If you cannot find five capable people to carry out these functions, perhaps you should not be running.)

8. Who are five people who will work the hardest to defeat you? (You should try to pinpoint those people

most likely to hurt you. In a primary especially, but even in a general election, they may be from your own party. Tactics should be devised to try to negate their impact or if possible to win them over. A leading campaign consultant recalls that one of his most successful clients told him that although pheasant was his favorite fowl, he'd eaten considerably more crow.)

9. What are the three major issues you will concentrate on? What is one basic strength and weakness of each issue? (Stick to three and keep them simple. More than three become confusing. Complicated issues are difficult for the average voter to grasp and identify with. The relative strengths and weaknesses of each issue must be weighed because any good issue will alienate, as well as attract, some group. You must carefully choose the issues which will attract the greatest number of votes for you. Although you obviously must be able to discuss a number of current issues intelligently when questioned, the campaign literature and publicity should stress the three chosen.)

After the candidate has completed such a self-appraisal, he should go over it with his closest advisers. What may seem to him to be a poor speaking style may not seem so bad to less sensitive, more neutral observers. Although the candidate's main concern may be with ecology issues, others may show him that the electorate is more worried about the economy.

Attention should also be paid to the opposition candidate. If he is an incumbent, his record should be carefully researched. The *Congressional Quarterly Weekly* and *Almanac* are good sources of valuable ammunition. The *Almanac* publishes over-all attendance records as well as a record and description of every vote each session. The *Weekly* contains descriptions of the week's congressional activities as well as a listing of every congressman's position on the week's roll-call and teller votes. From these sources, data can be compiled on the opponent's record on crucial issues. In addition, the *Congressional Record*, the official daily journal of Congress, should be checked for any foolish statements the opposition candidate may have made on the floor which could make good targets for campaign gibes.

The opponent's public appearances should also be monitored as closely as possible. This will allow your candidate's campaign to keep abreast of the issues he is concentrating on, to prepare rejoinders to charges he might be making about your candidate, and to insure that he is not altering his position on different issues to fit the audience. This doesn't mean harassing the opponent or engaging in Watergate-style skulduggery. Nor, most importantly, does it mean concentrating on his campaign to the point where you forget your own. Part of knowing yourself, however, is knowing what you are up against. There is nothing wrong about keeping close track of your opponent as long as it is done in a tasteful, sensible, *and* legal way; and as long as it does not divert you from the real themes and concerns of your own campaign.

RESEARCH

Nine of every ten volunteers will ask to do research. If allowed to go their own way, they will produce reams of detailed reports on topics ranging from the ABM to the price of eggs. During his brother's 1960 campaign for the presidency, Robert Kennedy developed a stock answer for those who came to him with offers to solve the problems of disarmament, poverty, and race relations. "Fine," Kennedy would say, "but can you lick stamps?" Licking stamps may be less fun, but it often produces more votes than much of the research effort that is likely to go into a campaign.

WHAT IS USEFUL RESEARCH   We do not mean to downgrade the importance of good research: few parts of the campaign are more important. What must be stressed is that *all research operations must be relevant to the major objective: winning the election*. One of the most important areas of research is the development of detailed profiles of the district. Polls, in this sense, are a fact of research. Indeed, a good poll can be conducted only on the basis of good preliminary research that locates major subgroups of the population and defines key issues and image problems.

PRACTICAL RESEARCH   The research staff works in close harmony with the rest of the campaign. It provides those working on registration with detailed district-by-district analyses of registration patterns, past voting behavior, and population characteristics. It provides canvassers with material on the kinds of attitudes they are likely to find in particular kinds of districts. And it carefully monitors and evaluates the record background and campaign of the opponent.

The research team must work closely with scheduling and campaigning to supply the background on where to go and what to say. Such seemingly trivial questions as what gate factory workers use, what time the candidate can best arrive at a dinner to avoid having to sit and listen to the other speakers, and what times are best for appearances at shopping centers can do much to conserve the most valuable resource of the campaign: the candidate himself.

ISSUE RESEARCH   Issue research can be divided into three categories. First, background briefing sessions with the candidate and other major figures in the campaign should be scheduled at least once a week and should begin early in the campaign. The purpose of these sessions is not simply to inform the candidate but also to keep research abreast of feedback from other campaign efforts. What kinds of questions are people asking during campaign appearances? What are the canvassers finding out about voters? About attitudes? How well are the brochures being received? Briefing sessions must begin very early in the campaign and cover a wide range of issues. Voters may not be well informed themselves, but they most certainly expect their politicians to be versed in current issues.

Second, research must be able to provide background papers on a selected range of key issues. A candidate must obviously be prepared to discuss inflation and similar issues of universal concern. Research must not, however, overlook issues of specialized concern to the district and to key subgroups within it. This effort may in fact be more important. In most cases, candidates have already developed their positions on many of the issues. Research can add little beyond frills and statistics, and these are likely to be beyond the competence or concern of most voters. The one group for which such research might be useful is the volunteers. It is important that they know the candidate's positions, and they are likely to be well enough informed to use detailed analyses. Long issue statements, however, are best saved for internal distribution.

While the research team is preparing background papers for the use of the campaign staff, it must also be keeping track of the opposition. The congressional records of most incumbents contain weak spots that can be exploited in the campaign: poor attendance, bad votes, or crucial absences.

The third key function of research is to prepare policy statements for brochures, speeches, and press releases. Most important is to prepare short statements on key issues. Ironically, many candidates will put in long hours working over a speech to be delivered before seventy-five Rotarians (most of whom have already made up their minds) and then turn around and give a radio broadcaster an uninformed, off-the-cuff statement that will be heard by 25,000. Every candidate should have committed to memory a short statement in answer to questions on any major issue that might arise. These can also be used by volunteers.

PUTTING IT ALL TOGETHER

One of the most difficult problems in a volunteer organization is the co-ordination and control of work. A campaign is not the place to "do your own thing." Teamwork is essential and priority schedules must be observed. Not everyone can do research; some must lick stamps. No canvasser, no matter how many previous campaigns he has worked in, should go into the field without a thorough briefing. No one at any stage or in any facet of the campaign should lose sight of the over-all goal of winning at least 50 per cent plus one of the votes cast.

Let us end this section, as we began Chapter 7, with a postelection visit to campaign headquarters, but in this case as the base of a victorious effort. Here, perhaps, are the same wasted coffee cups—looking a little better perhaps with the remains of victory champagne glistening in the bottom but still a waste of resources. Here are no leftover piles of literature—research and publicity were well-enough co-ordinated to get all pieces of literature delivered. There are no unusable photographs, no senseless gimmicks, priorities having been carefully set and adhered to.

Here, most important, is the victorious candidate. Will his record in Washington live up to expectations? Will he return for his next campaign strengthened by his experiences or wearied and frustrated by institutions that are too slow to respond and by problems that yield no easy solutions?

And here too is the team that put him in office. Where do they go from here?

184 VOTE POWER

NOTES

1. On the history and significance of such realignments, see Walter Dean Burnham, *Critical Elections and the Mainsprings of American Politics* (New York: Norton, 1970). On the nature of the emerging issue cleavages of the contemporary era, see Edward Schneier, "Intellectuals and the New Politics," *Bulletin of the Atomic Scientists,* October 1968, pp. 15–18.

2. One of the best single sources of new political technologies is James M. Perry, *The New Politics* (New York: Potter, 1968).

3. Ibid., p. 6.

4. Ithiel de Sola Pool, "TV, a New Dimension in Politics," in Eugene Burdick and A. J. Brodbeck, eds., *American Voting Behavior* (Glencoe, Ill.: Free Press, 1957), p. 241.

5. Harold Mendelsohn and Irving Crespi, *Polls, Television, and the New Politics* (Scranton, Penn.: Chandler, 1970), p. 252.

6. Ibid., p. 253.

7. Robert L. Peabody, Jeffrey M. Berry, William G. Frasure, and Jerry Goldman, *To Enact a Law: Congress and Campaign Financing* (New York: Praeger, 1972), p. 6.

8. Angus Campbell, et al., *The American Voter* (New York: Wiley, 1960), p. 322.

9. Dan Nimmo, *The Political Persuaders* (Englewood Cliffs, N.J.: Prentice-Hall, 1970), p. 141.

10. Quoted in Perry, op. cit., p. 53.

11. Nimmo, op. cit., p. 134.

12. Stein Rokkan, *Citizens, Elections, Parties* (Olso, Norway: Scandanavian University Books, 1970), pp. 423–24.

13. Ibid., p. 424.

14. Ibid.

15. Daniel Katz and Paul Lazarsfeld, *Personal Influence* (Glencoe, Ill.: Free Press, 1951).

16. Elmo Roper, *Emerging Profiles of Television and Other Mass Media* (New York: Television Information Office, 1967).

17. This, in rather simplified form, is the argument presented and very ably supported by Stanley Kelley, Jr., in "The Simple Act of Voting," a paper presented at the 1972 Annual Meeting of the American Political Science Association in Washington, D.C.

18. Walter DeVries, "Taking the Voter's Pulse," in Ray Hiebert, Robert Jones, John Lorenz, and Ernest Lotito, eds., *The Political Image Merchants* (Washington, D.C.: Acropolis Books, 1971), pp. 68–70.

19. Ibid., p. 64.

20. This list is adapted from one used by campaign consultant Hank Parkinson; see Parkinson, *Winning Your Campaign* (Englewood Cliffs, N.J.: Prentice-Hall, 1970), pp. 27–40.

CHAPTER 9

FOLLOWING THROUGH

The job is not finished, however, when Election Day has ended. Not only must preparations begin for the next election, but some steps must be taken to follow through on the work already begun. In Washington the real voice of the American people sounds strangely muted. The politician as campaigner and the politician as officeholder are different animals. But if constituents are to keep check on their representatives, they must know what their congressmen are talking about, how they can best approach him, and how they can hold him accountable for his actions.

MONITORING CONGRESS

How do you keep informed about what your congressman is doing? Mailings from the congressman's office must be taken with a grain of salt. They are political propaganda intended not to portray accurately the member's stand on a wide spectrum of issues but only to help his image with the voters.

Local newpapers seldom devote much space to a congressman's Washington activities, and therefore the political activist should be aware of the primary sources of such information, most of which are available in university or public libraries. A congressman's biography and committee assignments can be found in the current *Congressional Directory*. His record on roll-call votes is easily obtainable; two excellent publications, *Congressional Quarterly* and *National Journal*, publish weekly reports on all activities in Congress. Their simpler format and the condensed synopses presented for each vote make them more useful sources than the official one, the *Congressional Record*. In addition, at the end of each session the *Congressional Quarterly* weekly report provides several indexes by which you can rate your congressman's or senator's performance. Some of the most useful are "The Conservative Coalition Score," "Party Unity Score," "Presidential Support Score," "Expanding the Federal Role Score, Voting Participation Score. Ratings by four major interest groups—Americans for Democratic Action (ADA), the AFL-CIO's Committee on Political Education (COPE), National Farmer's Union (NFU), and Americans for Constitutional Action (ACA)—are also published in *Congressional Quarterly*. Listings of how senators and representatives voted on major issues are usually printed in the following day's edition of the Washington *Post*, which large libraries subscribe to.

The recent reorganization of the House of Representatives has helped to eliminate a procedure that allowed some members to cast "secret" votes on many crucial issues. Most voting in the House is now done while it sits as the Committee of the Whole House on the State of the Union, a parliamentary device intended to speed up and make less formal the House's business by reducing from 218 to 100 the number of members needed to constitute a quorum. While the House is sitting as the Committee of the Whole, issues are settled by voice votes, standing divisions, or teller votes. Before the recent changes it was very difficult to get an accurate list of how members vote on tellers, and some

members were thus able to vote in ways that would displease
their constituents were their votes known. Such secret votes
have been virtually done away with by instituting record
teller votes whereby clerks record each member's vote, which
are then reported in the *Congressional Record*.

In Chapter 2 we pointed out that most of the really important business of Congress is done in the committees. It
is there that legislation is drafted and much of the bargaining and compromise takes place. Until recently it was almost
impossible for the public to get any information about what
went on at the critical committee stage of the legislative process. The Legislative Reorganization Act of 1970 was supposed
to open committee doors. It has helped. Some previously un-
published records are now publicly available, but even as
recently as 1972 some 40 per cent of all committee business
meetings were still closed to public scrutiny—about the same
proportion as in the previous twenty years.

In early 1973 the Democratic Study Group spearheaded
an attempt to pry open committee doors and let the public
in. Representatives Bob Eckhardt (D., Texas) and Dante
B. Fascell (D., Florida) introduced legislation to keep all
House committee meetings open unless they dealt with national security or with personal character. A successful amendment to the legislation allows committees to vote in advance
to close their meetings if they so wish. As of mid-1973 the
new rules seemed to be working. Although a committee
majority could vote to close the meetings during the
"markup" stage (when legislation is revised, amended, and
the language finalized), almost all House committee meetings
remained open. This was not only a major victory for House
reformers but it also gives citizen groups an opportunity to
keep tabs on their representatives at a stage when their
behavior is probably more important than on roll-call votes.
This information remains much harder to find than information on roll calls, but the fact that it is available helps. It is
unfortunate, then, that the leadership of both parties in the

Senate, which generally held more open sessions than the House, killed a similar proposal for that body.

MAKING YOUR CONGRESSMAN MORE
EFFECTIVE

Unlike senators, members of the House of Representatives have very little assistance available for actual legislative work. Most of the time and energy of their Washington office staff must go into administrative problems, answering the mail, responding to constituents' requests for help and information, and carrying out similar non-legislative tasks. Beyond the issues dealt with by the committee to which he is assigned, the typical House member simply lacks the resources to consider new programs, much less to innovate them. The pressures of time are so great, moreover, that he has little opportunity to reflect on the larger questions of priorities, trends, and issue development. While administrative agencies, lobbies, and the member's colleagues can be counted upon to fill a part of this void, concerned consitutent groups might also be able to perform valuable services.

It is striking how rapidly campaign organizations dissolve. What happens to the research done during the campaign? Who is there to follow it up and turn campaign promises into specific proposals for legislative action? Citizens in every congressional district have valuable knowledge: knowledge of issues both local and national which congressmen could use. Yet the organizational vehicles for bringing congressmen together with these sources of advice and information cease to exist once a campaign ends. Perhaps successful candidates should give serious consideration to establishing, out of their campaign operations, continuing advisory bodies or "kitchen cabinets" to maintain these links. Not only could such groups make the member more effective in the House, they could also substantially enhance the possibilities of his re-election two years later when his record in Washington can become a campaign issue.

Even for defeated candidates, a group analogous to the British "shadow cabinet" might be set up to monitor continuously and comment upon the work of the victorious opponent. By the time a newly elected congressman takes office in January, his next campaign is only eighteen months away, and it is never too early to begin.

Information is only one of the many services that constituency groups can provide a congressman. Congressmen should be encouraged to try out their ideas and expound on their experiences before sympathetic but detached audiences at frequent intervals. For many members, however, such audiences are not easy to find. A congressman's visits to his district are ultimately shaped by the organizations that can provide him with audiences large enough to merit his time. His impressions of constituency opinion are therefore likely to be determined by the best organized of his constituents: chambers of commerce, Elks, Rotarians, veteran's groups, and so on. Special-interest groups also command a large part of his time. From his perspective, there will be many silent majorities and minorities who contributed to his campaign and then disappeared from view. To counter this, volunteer activists can serve an important role as supplementary eyes and ears for him in the district. The intelligence they gather on emerging issues of local importance or on key political developments can be very useful to him.

LOBBYING

The startling announcement of the invasion of Cambodia by American forces stirred thousands of citizens to go to Washington in the spring of 1970 to urge their congressmen to restrict this widening of the war. The earliest efforts were hit-or-miss, spur-of-the-moment attempts, but within weeks, well-organized lobbying efforts began to take place on Capitol Hill. For example, the Academic and Professional Alliance for a Responsible Congress recruited, briefed, and arranged appointments for delegations of businessmen, professors, lawyers, doctors, and other groups to press the case for peace with their representatives and senators. These well-planned visits undoubtedly contributed to the surprisingly large Senate vote for the Cooper-Church and Hatfield-McGovern amendments in 1970.

Without such planning, citizen lobbying can be more frustrating than productive. It would be hard to imagine another political activity in which so many have invested so much time and energy to get so little return. What many amateur lobbyists tend to forget is that members of Congress have minds of their own and are, as part of their job, surprisingly well informed about the major issues of the day.

If certain elementary ground rules are kept in mind, lobbying can tip the balance of a closely divided contest. If poorly planned and poorly executed, lobbying can actually do harm to a good cause. Here are some useful tips.

First of all, lobby your own congressman. Members care most about people who can vote for or against them. If you are from his district, and especially if you are identified with some electoral organization that actually puts workers into the field, you will probably get a respectful hearing. If you are not from the district, other means of entree—from old school ties to common issue concerns—may help open the door.

This respect can disappear very quickly, however, if you display little knowledge of the member's publicly stated positions on the issues or if the legislation on which you are lobbying was voted on two months ago or will not be voted on until six months from now. Do your homework and realize that Congress, particularly the House, is an institution that emphasizes division of labor and specialization. Do not expect a member of the Agriculture Committee to be terribly worried (or informed) about the Head Start program, or a member of the Education and Labor Committee to be very interested in farm subsidy programs. In the same vein, a constituent who, in a letter or visit, displays specialized expertise on some particular problem which is of interest to the congressman will be respected and receive a good hearing. If you are going to Washington to talk to a congressman or congressmen about a public policy matter, you should make sure that you are thoroughly familiar with both the issue at hand and the position of the member or members you plan to contact.

All studies of lobbying show that it is most effective when carried out as a reinforcement rather than conversion process. A member can feel much more secure in taking positions when he knows, or has been led to believe, that substantial support for his position exists among the political elites of his district. Such selective lobbying can also sometimes raise an issue from low to high visibility in the eyes of a congressman. A congressman or senator who is known to be leaning toward your position but is still sitting on the fence can sometimes be brought over by a well-organized effort. If he receives 1,000 well-written letters on the subject, he might be won over. On the other hand, nothing raises congressional hackles quicker than massive form-letter write-in campaigns in which 5,000 of the 10,000 letters begin, "Dear Congressman Write in Name of Your Representative Here." For good reason, most congressmen perceive such letters as the product of weak minds and powerful mimeo machines and accordingly assign them to the circular file.

Lobbying organizations can be most effective when directed at specific targets, such as the Cooper-Church and Hatfield-McGovern amendments to end American military involvement in the war in Southeast Asia. However, even such specifically oriented groups as these encountered terrific difficulties when legislation shifted from the Senate to the House and the number of "undecided" members to be lobbied jumped from fifteen or twenty quite identifiable senators to eighty or a hundred essentially unknown congressmen. A substantial army of volunteers is needed even to keep track of the many shades and nuances of House opinion and of shifts in voting blocs and alliances within so large and unwieldy a body. It is particularly easy in the House to be "booby-trapped" by technicalities in rules and procedures. Careful organization and briefing on these matters are pre-requisite of effective lobbying in the House on a major issue.

Both in Washington and at the grass roots, a technique that is often effective is to lobby existing groups like the AFL-CIO, trade associations, or professional societies, in order to get them to put their resources (which are usually better organized) to work on doing the actual lobbying in Washington. This is much less expensive for citizen activists and may result in the formation of local alliances that can be very worthwhile in future elections. Student lobbyists have had considerable success in using college alumni con-tacts to give them entree into existing groups within con-gressional districts throughout the country.

Lobbying and electoral activity are two sides of the same coin. The congressman pays more attention to lobbyists from his constituency if he knows that new forces are stirring back home in the district and that the lobbyists were manning the barricades for him when it counted—in the election. Much of the time spent in lobbying activities, particularly when it is random and ill co-ordinated, could be spent much more profitably in direct electoral action. Fifty students spending two hours in a rap session with some congressman will probably have little effect on his views. Yet if those hundred man-hours were spent doing precinct work in his district, there would be a much higher prob-ability that he might move closer to your position, or even adopt it.

The effectiveness of a lobbying effort is frequently in in-verse ratio to the national significance of the issue. Your letter on any issue is likely to be seen only as one of thousands on both sides of the question representing a biased sample of constituency opinion. But a carefully considered discussion on a little discussed issue or one of largely local concern may in itself be sufficient to produce action. Good lobbying is seen by a congressman as a service: it provides information he could not otherwise get. Even this kind of lobbying, however, is most effective when it is backed by the potential promise of effective campaign activity when he comes up for re-election.

The most effective lobbyist of all, most congressmen will admit, is an informed and respected colleague. Thus, mobilizing those friendly to your cause is an important lobbying strategy. It depends, however, upon finding the right target: those members who enjoy the greatest respect and prestige within the legislature on the issues you are interested in.

FOLLOWING THROUGH IN THE DISTRICT

Politics is hard work. Tedious meetings and boring jobs are part of the package. These, however, are the prices of power. To those who persist, who are not political morning glories, the prizes are there for the taking. The time to begin is now. Campaign '76 has already begun.

A number of campaigns being waged in 1974 will have a bearing on the outcome in 1976. Tomorrow's candidates for Congress may be running today for state or local office. And the results in certain key states will be carefully watched for clues to the presidential race in 1976. What happens in 1974 is important, but few political outcomes are permanent. If the forces pushing for change can demonstrate staying power as well as enthusiasm, the system will change.

The American party system is structured from the bottom up. There is no centralized control. That is why it is possible for conservative Senators Strom Thurmond of South Carolina and liberal Senator Jacob Javits of New York both to consider themselves loyal Republicans, why conservative Senator James Eastland of Mississippi and liberal Senator George McGovern of South Dakota are both Democrats. If the source of political power can be traced in our two parties it could be seen to emanate from the very smallest units—precinct and district captains, ward leaders and county chairmen—these are the men who run our political parties. Yet many districts have no leaders because no one is interested in running. Others have figureheads who do no work and could be defeated easily. Still others are so out of touch with contemporary realities as to be worse than none at all. In 1962 and 1963 thousands of these seemingly insignificant posts were won by hard-line conservatives who were looking ahead to 1964. It was their hard work that put such non-primary states as Washington into the Goldwater column at the 1964 Republican National Convention. Similar efforts by liberals won the Democratic presidential nomination for George McGovern in 1972.

WORKING TOWARD A NEW POLITICS

Individual citizens can have an impact on the political process. To do so, they must be willing to work hard and to channel their efforts into effective forms of activity. Congress is an important part of our political system, but it is only a part. A new Congress alone cannot guarantee peace or a reordering of national priorities. Nor will the newly elected members in 1974 fulfill the bright hopes of their supporters unless they are given continuing motives for doing so. Only you can decide how much or how little of that support and that pressure will be brought to bear.

THE NINETY-NINE MOST MARGINAL
HOUSE DISTRICTS

Listed below are those districts in which the incumbent received less than 57 per cent of the vote in the 1972 election. In some of these districts special factors, such as multiparty candidacies, actually make a district a "safe" one. An example is New York's 20th District. Although Bella Abzug received slightly less than 56 per cent of the total votes cast, she beat her closest challenger by over 27 per cent. The special circumstances of redistricting, incumbency, the death of an incumbent, and multiparty candidacies all played a role. Obviously, it is impossible in a listing of this sort to take into consideration all the factors peculiar to any particular election. Such factors should be weighed seriously, however, by the activist before he decides how and where to commit his energies.

NOTE

1. Republicans' names are in italics, the others are either Democratic or Independent.
2. Asterisks denote multiparty races as follows:
    * three candidates
    ** four candidates
    *** five candidates
3. Last column represents percentage margin of victory over nearest challenger.

	Incumbent (state, district)	Per cent of vote	Victory margin
1.	Moakley (Mass., 9)	43.2	2.1**
2.	*Parris* (Va., 8)	44.4	5.6**
3.	*Daniel* (Va., 4)	47.1	9.6***
4.	*Cochran* (Miss., 4)	47.8	3.8**
5.	*Gilman* (N.Y., 26)	47.8	8.5*
6.	Drinan (Mass., 4)	48.8	3.0*
7.	*Minshall* (Ohio, 23)	49.4	2.1*
8.	Studds (Mass., 12)	50.3	0.6
9.	*Pritchard* (Wash., 1)	50.3	1.2*
10.	*Peyser* (N.Y., 23)	50.4	0.8
11.	Andrews (N.C., 4)	50.4	0.8
12.	*Froelich* (Wis., 8)	50.4	1.9*
13.	*Chamberlain* (Mich., 6)	50.6	1.2
14.	O'Hara (Mich., 12)	50.8	1.6
15.	*Johnson* (Colo., 4)	51.0	2.0
16.	*Zwach* (Minn., 6)	51.0	2.0
17.	*Mitchell* (N.Y., 31)	51.0	11.9**
18.	*Sarasin* (Conn., 5)	51.2	2.4
19.	*Hudnut* (Ind., 11)	51.2	2.4
20.	Roush (Ind., 4)	51.5	3.0
21.	Wolff (N.Y., 6)	51.5	3.0
22.	*Young* (Ill., 10)	51.6	3.2
23.	Schroeder (Colo., 1)	51.6	4.1
24.	Roncalio (Wyo., at large)	51.7	3.4
25.	*Treen* (La., 3)	51.8	3.6
26.	*Mailliard* (Calif., 6)	52.1	4.2
27.	McCormack (Wash., 4)	52.1	4.2
28.	Carey (N.Y., 15)	52.1	9.1**
29.	*Powell* (Ohio, 8)	52.2	4.4
30.	*Towell* (Nev., at large)	52.2	4.4
31.	Reid (N.Y., 24)	52.2	4.4
32.	*Young* (Alaska, at large)	52.3	4.6
33.	Patten (N.J., 15)	52.3	4.6

	Incumbent (state, district)	Per cent of vote	Victory margin
34.	Wilson (Calif., 31)	52.3	9.8*
35.	Breckinridge (Ky., 6)	52.4	5.6*
36.	*Mayne* (Iowa, 6)	52.5	5.0
37.	*Hunt* (N.J., 1)	52.5	5.4***
38.	Pike (N.Y., 1)	52.5	15.6**
39.	*Huber* (Mich., 18)	52.6	5.2
40.	*Ketchum* (Calif., 36)	52.7	9.2*
41.	Young (Ga., 5)	52.8	5.6
42.	Stark (Calif., 8)	52.9	5.8
43.	*Conlan* (Ariz., 4)	53.0	6.0
44.	Howard (N.J., 3)	53.0	6.0
45.	*Roncallo* (N.Y., 3)	53.1	15.5**
46.	Giaimo (Conn., 3)	53.3	6.6
47.	Annunzio (Ill., 11)	53.3	6.6
48.	Mezvinsky (Iowa, 1)	53.4	7.7*
49.	*Cronin* (Mass., 5)	53.5	8.8*
50.	*Shoup* (Mont., 1)	53.7	7.4
51.	Rooney (N.Y., 14)	53.9	25.8**
52.	*Treen* (La., 3)	54.0	8.0
53.	*Talcott* (Calif., 12)	54.0	10.9*
54.	*Cohen* (Me., 2)	54.4	8.8
55.	*Young* (S.C., 6)	54.4	8.8
56.	Davis (S.C., 1)	54.5	9.0
57.	Owens (Utah, 2)	54.5	10.5*
58.	Jones (Okla., 1)	54.5	10.8
59.	Litton (Mo., 6)	54.6	9.2
60.	*Butler* (Va., 6)	54.5	15.4*
61.	*McCloskey* (Calif., 17)	54.6	18.7*
62.	Matsunaga (Hawaii, 1)	54.7	9.4
63.	*Landgrebe* (Ind., 2)	54.7	9.4
64.	*Thomson* (Wis., 3)	54.8	10.1*
65.	*Madigan* (Ill., 21)	54.8	9.6
66.	*Price* (Texas, 13)	54.8	9.6

	Incumbent (state, district)	Per cent of vote	Victory margin
67.	*Dickinson* (Ala., 2)	54.8	13.3**
68.	Nedzi (Mich., 14)	54.9	9.8
69.	*Abdnor* (S.D., 2)	54.9	9.8
70.	Brademas (Ind., 3)	55.2	12.0*
71.	*Baker* (Tenn., 3)	55.2	13.3
72.	*Scherle* (Iowa, 5)	55.3	10.6
73.	*Lott* (Miss., 5)	55.3	11.1
74.	*Beard* (Tenn., 6)	55.4	12.2*
75.	*Kuykendall* (Tenn., 8)	55.4	11.3*
76.	McKay (Utah, 1)	55.4	13.4*
77.	Gunter (Fla., 5)	55.5	11.0
78.	*O'Brien* (Ill., 17)	55.6	11.2
79.	*Symms* (Idaho, 1)	55.6	11.2
80.	*Gross* (Iowa, 3)	55.7	11.4
81.	*Lujan* (N.M., 1)	55.7	11.4
82.	*Steelman* (Texas, 5)	55.7	11.4
83.	*Maraziti* (N.J., 13)	55.7	12.8
84.	Abzug (N.Y., 20)	55.7	27.7***
85.	Helstoski (N.J., 9)	55.8	11.6
86.	Clark (Penn., 25)	55.8	11.6
87.	Chappell (Fla., 4)	55.9	11.8
88.	Eilberg (Penn., 4)	55.9	11.8
89.	Brown (Calif., 38)	55.9	12.5*
90.	Dellums (Calif., 7)	55.9	17.8*
91.	*Esch* (Mich., 2)	56.0	12.7*
92.	*Devine* (Ohio, 12)	56.1	12.2
93.	*Broyhill* (Va., 10)	56.3	12.6
94.	*Johnson* (Penn., 23)	56.5	13.0
95.	Shipley (Ill., 22)	56.5	15.5*
96.	Fascell (Fla., 15)	56.8	13.6
97.	Fisher (Texas, 21)	56.8	13.6
98.	Madden (Ind., 1)	56.9	13.8
99.	Cotter (Conn., 1)	56.9	15.0*

THE LEADERSHIP OF THE 93RD CONGRESS AS OF NOVEMBER 1973

SENATE

Democrats

President Pro Tempore	James O. Eastland (Miss.)
Majority Leader	Mike Mansfield (Mont.)
Majority Whip	Robert C. Byrd (W.Va.)
Conference Chairman	Mike Mansfield (Mont.)
Policy Committee Chairman	Mike Mansfield (Mont.)
Steering Committee Chairman	Mike Mansfield (Mont.)
Campaign Committee Chairman	Ernest F. Hollings (S.C.)

Republicans

Minority Leader	Hugh Scott (Penn.)
Minority Whip	Robert P. Griffin (Mich.)
Conference Chairman	Norris Cotton (N.H.)
Conference Secretary	Wallace F. Bennett (Utah)
Policy Committee Chairman	John G. Tower (Texas)
Committee on Committees Chairman	Jacob K. Javits (N.Y.)
Campaign Committee Chairman	William E. Brock, 3rd (Tenn.)

HOUSE

Democrats

Speaker	Carl Albert (Okla.)
Majority Leader	Thomas P. O'Neill, Jr. (Mass.)
Majority Whip	John J. McFall (Calif.)
Deputy Whip	John Brademas (Ind.)
Caucus Chairman	Olin E. Teague (Texas)
Caucus Secretary	Leonor K. Sullivan (Mo.)
Campaign Committee Chairman	Wayne L. Hays (Ohio)
Steering and Policy Committee Chmn.	Carl Albert (Okla.)
Patronage Committee Chairman	Thomas E. Morgan (Penn.)

Republicans

Minority Leader	Gerald R. Ford (Mich.)
Minority Whip	Leslie C. Arends (Ill.)
Conference Chairman	John B. Anderson (Ill.)
Conference Vice-Chairman	Samuel L. Devine (Ohio)
Conference Secretary	Jack Edwards (Ala.)
Policy Committee Chairman	John J. Rhodes (Ariz.)
Committee on Committees	Gerald R. Ford (Mich.)
Campaign Committee Chairman	Robert H. Michel (Ill.)
Research Committee Chairman	Barber B. Conable (N.Y.)

REGISTRATION LAWS
AND ABSENTEE BALLOTING PROCEDURES
IN THE FIFTY STATES*

	Residence Requirements	Registration Deadline		Where to Register
		primary	*general*	
Alabama	30 days	10 days before election	10 days before election	County Court House
Alaska	30 days	30 days before election	30 days before election	state election office, city & borough clerk, precinct registrar
Arizona	50 days	50 days before election	50 days before election	County Recorder, Justice of the Peace, volunteer registration sites
Arkansas	30 days	20 days before election	20 days before election	Registrar of County

*Latest figures as of September 15, 1973, as supplied by the National Office of the League of Women Voters.

Who Can Vote Absentee (*see note 2*)	Where to Obtain Absentee Ballot	Deadline for Request	Party Affiliation (*deadline for declaration of party to vote in primary*)
a, b, c, those away regularly on business	Registrar of Civil Circuit Court	5 days before election	no prior affiliation required
a, b, c, d, e, anyone away from polls on elec. day	Lt. Governor, Magistrate, election supervisor	6 mos. to 4 days before election	open primary
a, b, c, d, e	County Recorder	within 30 days preceding Sat. before elec.	50 days before election
anyone unavoidably away from polling place; disabled or ill	County Clerk	1 day before election	no prior affiliation required

	Residence Requirements	Registration Deadline		Where to Register
		primary	*general*	
California	30 days	30 days before election	30 days before election	anywhere in city before Deputy Registrar, firehouses, office of Registrar of Voters
Colorado	32 days	32 days before election	32 days before election	County Clerk's Office
Connecticut	(*see note 1*)		Sat. of 4th week before election	Town Clerk or Registrar of Voters, session of Bd. of Admission of Electors, public sessions
Delaware	(*see note 1*)	21 days before election	3rd Sat. in Oct.	central registration in county, mobile registration (in home district 4th Sat. in July & 3rd Sat. in Oct.— elec. yrs.)
Florida	60 days	30 days before election	30 days before election	Court House, with Supervisor of Elections, or branch offices

Who Can Vote Absentee (*see note 2*)	Where to Obtain Absentee Ballot	Deadline for Request	Party Affiliation (*deadline for declaration of party to vote in primary*)
c, d, anyone unable to get to poll election day	Registrar of Voters, County Clerk	7th day before election	30 days before election
a, b, c, d, e	County Clerk	5:00 P.M. Fri. before election	election day if not now affiliated; change, by 32 days before election
a, b, c, anyone absent from state, religious reasons, illness	Town Clerk	day before election	new voter: day before; unafffiliated voter: next enrollment session; change: 6 months
a, b, c, d, e	County Dept. of Elections	noon—day before election	March 1 of election year
a, b, c, d	Supervisor of Elections	5 P.M. day before election	close of registration books

	Residence Requirements	Registration Deadline		Where to Register
		primary	*general*	
Georgia	—	50 days before election	50 days before election	County Board of Registrars
Hawaii	—	4:30 P.M. 30th day before election	4:30 P.M. 26th day before election	City Clerk's office, City Hall; election yrs. with Lt. Gov.'s ofc., house to house reg.
Idaho	(*see note 1*)	2 days before election	2 days before election	County Clerk or Precinct Registrar
Illinois	30 days	30 days before election	30 days before election	City Hall or during precinct registration days
Indiana	60 days (township)	29th day before election	29th day before election	Office of Registration Board, Clerk of Circuit Court, before deputy registrar
Iowa	—	10th day before election	10th day before election	Office of County Commissioner, or with deputy
Kansas	20 days	20 days before election	20 days before election	County Election Commissioner's office, County Court House, City Hall

Who Can Vote Absentee (*see note 2*)	Where to Obtain Absentee Ballot	Deadline for Request	Party Affiliation (*deadline for declaration of party to vote in primary*)
a, b, c, d, e, election officials	County Board of Registrars	90 days before elections	at poll
a, b, c, d, e, anyone living more than 10 miles from polls	City or County Clerk's office	4:30 P.M., 7th day before election	choose party ballot at primary, which becomes his party
a, b, c, d, e	County Clerk	1 day before election	declare party before voting
a, e, those observing religious holiday	Board or Election Commissioners	30 days to 5 days before election	no previous affiliation required
e, those confined due to illness or injury	County Election Board	Sat. before election	declare party when voting
a, b, c, d, e	County Commissioner	day before election	no previous party affiliation required
a, b, c, d, e	County Election Commission	5 days before election	day of primary if not affiliated; change, 20 days before

| | Residence Requirements | Registration Deadline | | Where to Register |
		primary	*general*	
Kentucky	—	30 days before election	30 days before election (45 days in 1973)	County Clerk's office or special registration sites
Louisiana	—	30 days before election	30 days before election	office of Registrar of Parish
Maine	—	election day	election day	before Registrar of Voters, Board or Registration, Justice of Peace, or Notary Public
Maryland	28 days	28 days before election	28 days before election	Local Election Board, out of office registration sites, by mail some places
Massachusetts	31 days	31 days before election (mun. el. 20 days)	31 days before election (mun. el. 20 days)	City or Town Hall in Office of Registrar or Election Commissioner

Who Can Vote Absentee (*see note 2*)	Where to Obtain Absentee Ballot	Deadline for Request	Party Affiliation (*deadline for declaration of party to vote in primary*)
a, b, d, e	County Clerk	7 days before election	before preceding gen'l election; new voters 30 days before primary
c & spouse, merchant marines, civilian U.S. employees overseas, religious & welfare orgs. with armed forces	New Orleans: Civil Sheriff, Parishes: Clerk of Court	between 60th & 7th day before election	30 days before election
a, b, c, d, e	Town, City or Plantation Clerk	none	3 months before election
a, b, c, d, e, emergency ballot for illness or death in immediate family	local election board	7 days before election; emergency ballots to election day	change 4 months before election; new voter—before close of registration
a, e	City or Town Clerk or Election Commissioner	noon of day before election	declare party at poll; change 31 days before election

	Residence Requirements	Registration Deadline *primary*	Registration Deadline *general*	Where to Register
Michigan	(*see note 3*)	5th Fri. before election	5th Fri. before election	City or Township Clerk
Minnesota	30 days	20 days before election reg. elec. day w/ identification	same as primary	City Hall or other public place designated by official, or at poll election day
Mississippi	30 days	30 days before election	30 days before election	County Registrar or City Clerk
Missouri	30 days	28 days before election	28 days before election	County Clerk's Office & Office of Board of Election Commissioners
Montana	30 days	—	—	County Clerk & Recorder's Office, with deputy registrar or notary public
Nebraska	2nd Fri. before election	2nd Fri. before election	2nd Fri. before election	County Clerk or Election Commissioner

Who Can Vote Absentee (see note 2)	Where to Obtain Absentee Ballot	Deadline for Request	Party Affiliation (deadline for declaration of party to vote in primary)
a, b, c, d, e	local clerk	2 P.M. Sat. before election	no previous affiliation required
a, b, c, d, e	County Auditor	1 day before election	no party registration
a, b, c, anyone out of county for occupational reasons	County Registrar & City Clerk	in order to meet deadline for receipt of ballot	not applicable
a, c, d	County Clerk & Board of Election Commissioners	4th day before election	none
e	County Clerk & Recorder (st. or co. elecs) Municipal Clerk (mun. elecs.)	varies	no party registration
a, b, c, d, e	County Clerk or Election Commissioner	4 P.M. Fri. before election	no previous affiliation required

	Residence Requirements	Registration Deadline		Where to Register
		primary	*general*	
Nevada	30 days (*see note 3*)	5th Sat. before election	5th Sat. before election	Office of County Clerk Registrar of Voters, Justice of Peace, or volunteer deputy registrar
New Hampshire	30 days	—	—	Board of Supervisors of the Checklist
New Jersey	40 days	40 days before election	40 days before election	County Board or Elections of Office of Municipal Clerk
New Mexico	42 days	30 days before election	30 days before election	Office of County Clerk or by deputy registrar
New York	30 days	30 days before— "special enrollment"	10-13-73	County Board of Elections, at local polling places 2-3 days

Who Can Vote Absentee (see note 2)	Where to Obtain Absentee Ballot	Deadline for Request	Party Affiliation (deadline for declaration of party to vote in primary)
a, b, c, d	County Clerk	Tues. before election	30 days before election
a, b, c, d, e, ill	Town or City Clerk	any time before election	90 days before election; independents may declare at polls
a, b, c, d, all temporarily out of state	County Clerk	7 days before election	no previous affiliation required
a, b, c, d, e	County Clerk	10 days before election	30 days before election
a, b, c, d, vacationers & their spouse, parent, or children	County Board of Elections	—	30 days before previous gen. election; special enrollment 30 days before primary

	Residence Requirements	Registration Deadline		Where to Register
		primary	*general*	
North Carolina	30 days	30 days before prev. gen'l elec. 21 business days before election	21 business days before el.	Office of County Board of Elections
North Dakota	30 days	no registration	—	—
Ohio	30 days	30 days before election	30 days before election	Office of Board of Elections or outside registration area
Oklahoma	(*see note 1*)	7 days before election	7 days before election	County Election Board or Office of Deputy Registrar
Oregon	(*see note 1*)	31 days before election	31 days before election	County Clerk's Office or any official Registrar's office

Who Can Vote Absentee (*see note 2*)	Where to Obtain Absentee Ballot	Deadline for Request	Party Affiliation (*deadline for declaration of party to vote in primary*)
a, b, c, d, e	Executive Secretary or Chairman of Election Board		21 business days before election
a, b, c, d, e	County Auditor	day before election	no previous affiliation required
a, b, c, d, e, state employees, those observing religious beliefs	Board of Elections	4 P.M.—5 days before election	choose party at poll for 1st primary; vote in same one thereafter or swear to voting for majority of other party in last gen'l election
a, c, e, residents living temporarily abroad	Secretary of County Election Board	Fri. before election	no time requirement, but must be registered with party
a, b, c, d, e, anyone unable to get to polls election day	County Clerk	8 P.M. election day	31 days before election

| | Residence Requirements | Registration Deadline | | Where to Register |
		primary	*general*	
Pennsylvania	30 days	30 days before election	30 days before election	Court House, field registration at various times
Rhode Island	30 days	30 days before election	30 days before election	Local Board of Canvassers
South Carolina	30 days	30 days before election	30 days before election	County Board of Voter Registration Office
South Dakota	—	15 days before election	15 days before election	City of County Auditor, Township or Town Clerk
Tennessee	30 days	30 days before election	29 days before election	County Election Commission Office or with precinct registrar
Texas	31 days	31 days before election	31 days before election	County Tax Assessor-Collector

Who Can Vote Absentee (see note 2)	Where to Obtain Absentee Ballot	Deadline for Request	Party Affiliation (deadline for declaration of party to vote in primary)
a, b, c, d, e	County Board of Elections	5 P.M. Tues. before elec.; emergency application, 5 P.M. Fri. before	30 days before election
a, those outside the state	Secretary of State	21 days before election	no previous affiliation required
a, b, c, certain transportation workers	County Registration office, County Election Commission	no fixed date	no previous affiliation required
all eligible voters	County Auditor	15 days before election	must be in registration book at time of election or have duplicate registration card
any qualified voter who'd otherwise be unable to vote	County Election Commission	7 days before election	no previous affiliation required
e, a—with dr's certificate	County Clerk	—	no previous affiliation required

	Residence Requirements	Registration Deadline		Where to Register
		primary	*general*	
Utah	1st Tues. before election	1st Tues. before election	1st Tues. before election	County Clerk's Office or with registration agent
Vermont	(*see note 4*)	3 to 30 days before election	3 to 30 days before election	Town or City Clerk and Local Board of Civil Authority
Virginia	30 days	30 days before election	30 days before election	in presence of general registrar of city or county
Washington	30 days	30 days before election	30 days before election	County Auditor's Office, deputy registrars, City & Town Clerks
West Virginia	30 days	30 days before election	30 days before election	Office of Clerk of the County Court

Who Can Vote Absentee (*see note 2*)	Where to Obtain Absentee Ballot	Deadline for Request	Party Affiliation (*deadline for declaration of party to vote in primary*)
a, b, c, d, e	County Clerk	within 30 days of election	a, b, c, d, e
everyone legally registered	Town or City Clerk	4 days before election	no previous affiliation required
a, b, c, U.S. employees working overseas. Anyone temporarily out of county—in person only	in person—registrar or Sec. of Electoral Board. by mail—Sec. of Electoral Board	5 days before elec. by mail; 3 days in person	no party affiliation
a, b, c, d, e, anyone who can't vote personally for religious reasons	County Auditor	day before election	no party primary
a, b, c, d, e, anyone required to be absent during voting hrs.	Clerk of the Circuit Court	4th day before election	30 days before election

	Residence Require- ments	Registration Deadline		Where to Register
		primary	*general*	
Wisconsin	10 days	2nd Wed. before elec. Large cities 3rd Wed.	same as primary	Municipal Clerk of Board of Election Commissioners
Wyoming	(*see note 1*)	30 days before election	30 days before election	City or County Clerk's Office
DC	30 days	30 days before election	30 days before election	District Building, D.C. Public Libraries & other designated places
Puerto Rico	1 year	April	March	school

Who Can Vote Absentee (see note 2)	Where to Obtain Absentee Ballot	Deadline for Request	Party Affiliation (deadline for declaration of party to vote in primary)
anyone unable to vote in person due to illness, jury duty, or religious reasons, or if moved within state & didn't change registration	Municipal Clerk	5 P.M. Fri. before elec.—by mail; day before—in person	no previous affiliation required
a, b, c, d, e	County Clerk	before election day	may register at polls
a, b, c, d, e	Board of Elections	7 days before election	30 days before election
	General Supervisor of Elections	30 days before election	before last registration in April

NOTES

1. No durational residence requirements.

2. Letters in this column refer to: (a) disabled persons; (b) students; (c) military persons; (d) those away on business; (e) all those temporarily outside the county.

3. In Michigan, residency requirements vary for state, county, or precinct as follows: state is 45 days, county 30 days, precinct fifth Friday before the election; in Nevada: state and county requirements are 30 days, precinct requirement is 10 days.

4. In Vermont, residency requirements vary from 3 to 30 days with local board.